Phonics

Getting it right ✓

IN A WEEK

Angela Gill & David Waugh
Series editor: **Susan Wallace**

First published in 2017 by Critical Publishing Ltd

British Library Cataloguing in Publication Data

A CIP record for this book is available from the British Library

ISBN: 978-1-911106-34-0

This book is also available in the following e-book format:
MOBI: 978-1-911106-35-7

The rights of Angela Gill and David Waugh to be identified as the Authors of this work have been asserted by them in accordance with the Copyright, Design and Patents Act 1988.

Cartoons © (2017) Michael Wallace
Cover and text design by Out of House Limited
Project management by Out of House Publishing Solutions

Typeset by Out of House Publishing Solutions
Printed and bound in Great Britain by TJ International, Padstow, Cornwall

Critical Publishing
3 Connaught Road
St Albans
AL3 5RX

www.criticalpublishing.com

For orders and details of our bulk discounts please go to our website www.criticalpublishing.com or contact our distributor NBN International by telephoning 01752 202301 or emailing orders@nbninternational.com.

CONTENTS

Angela Gill

I am a former classteacher who worked for more than 20 years in primary schools in County Durham, Bath and North East Somerset. For many of those years I was subject leader for English and, in more recent years, for phonics. In January 2016 I joined Durham University, where I work as part of the primary English team teaching undergraduate and PGCE courses. My recent publications include books and articles about teaching systematic synthetic phonics and common exception words.

David Waugh

I am a former deputy headteacher who worked in initial teacher education (ITE) from 1990 at the University of Hull, where I led the PGCE course and became head of department. In 2008 I was appointed as a National Strategies Regional Adviser for ITE. I am currently Associate Professor at Durham University, where I am also subject leader for English. I have published extensively in primary English, as well as developing e-learning resources for National Strategies for English, mathematics and mentoring and coaching. I am the author of five children's novels.

Susan Wallace

I am Emeritus Professor of Education at Nottingham Trent University where part of my role has been to support trainee teachers on initial and in-service teacher training courses. My own experience of classroom teaching has been mainly with 14 to 19 year olds; and I have also worked in a local authority advisory role for this age group. My particular interest is in the motivation and behaviour management of reluctant and disengaged learners, and I've written a number of books and research papers on this topic. My work allows me the privilege of meeting, observing and listening to teachers from all sectors of education. It is to them that I owe many of the tips and ideas contained in these pages.

Acknowledgements

We would like to thank all of the teachers and trainee teachers who provided case study examples of their teaching for the strategy in action sections.

Introduction

Systematic synthetic phonics (SSP) has been central to the teaching of early reading since the Rose Review of 2006. It is one of only two elements of the curriculum which trainee teachers must be able to teach in order to achieve the Teachers' Standards (DfE, 2011a). Teachers' Standard 3 includes the following: *'if teaching early reading, demonstrate a clear understanding of systematic synthetic phonics'*.

SSP is a key element in Ofsted inspections of both schools and teacher training providers. In England, virtually all Key Stage 1 learners are taught phonics in schools and all Key Stage 1 learners take a phonics screening test. In addition, spelling, which involves phonic awareness, has been given greater emphasis in the 2014 national curriculum. Phonics is, therefore, a key element of primary education.

Designed to be read over seven days, the book is divided into seven practical chapters. It offers a range of tried and tested strategies for developing an understanding of phonics and effective pedagogy.

Each strategy is contained on one double page. The strategy page will include a *Strategy in action* section, illustrating how and when the strategy could be applied. Many of the strategies are divided into two or more sub-strategies so that you can find out about different aspects of each topic. There are usually brief summaries of the theory underpinning the strategy contained in a text box headed *A Spot of Theory*. There are several of these in each chapter. This feature, together with the *Further reading* listed at the end of the book, provides an introduction to relevant research for readers who wish to learn more about the relevant theoretical background, or who wish to reference it for their studies.

Towards the end of each chapter, you will find a section headed *If you only try one thing, try this*. If you are very short of time, you can go to this heading to find one suggested strategy out of the many given in each chapter. Finally, each chapter closes with a checklist of strategies in a grid format, which enables you to note down how well each strategy worked, who you tried it with and whether you would use it again.

The seven daily chapters follow a logical progression from focusing on early phonological development to looking at phonics at Key Stage 2. Day 1 provides a range of strategies for developing phonological awareness and teaching graphemes and phonemes. These are the basics of systematic synthetic phonics. Day 2 looks at basic decoding (reading) and encoding (spelling). Day 3 looks at digraphs and large grapheme units where more than one letter is used to make a phoneme (sound), while Day 4 looks at how we can teach common exception words: those words which don't conform to regular grapheme-phoneme correspondences. On Day 5 you will find guidance on systematic teaching, with a focus on planning and assessment; it also explores a range of popular phonics programmes that are commonly used in many primary schools. Day 6 presents strategies for teaching and learning spelling. The final day, Day 7, looks at phonics beyond Key Stage 1 and includes guidance on teaching more advanced grapheme-phoneme correspondences.

This book is designed to be easily read, easy to use and easy to relate to your own practice and experience. Its ultimate purpose is to help you to teach phonics well.

DAY 1: Grapheme-phoneme correspondence

Introduction

Today we will look at the basics of phonics. You will explore some of the activities which learners need to engage in before they begin to match letters to sounds, and will go on to look at some of the first things you can do to help them understand that letter sounds can be written down and that the letters can be read and made into words.

You will encounter some key vocabulary, including *phoneme* and *grapheme*, and *phonological awareness* and *phonemic awareness*, as well as some of the terms which you will meet later in the book, including *digraph, trigraph* and *quadgraph*. We emphasise from Day 1 the importance of making phonics engaging and interactive and using a rich language environment to surround learners with opportunities to develop their language and literacy skills. This includes providing lots of opportunities for them to hear and join in with stories, poems, songs and rhymes so that they can enjoy language and see how it works and what they will be able to do as they develop their skills and knowledge.

Today's strategies

- Developing phonological awareness:
  1. What activities can you use to develop phonological awareness?
  2. How do learners acquire sounds?

- Identifying phonemes:
  3. What is a phoneme?
  4. How can you develop phonemic awareness?

- Identifying graphemes:
  5. What is a grapheme?
  6. How can you represent the 44 phonemes?
  7. What are alternative graphemes?

- The importance of clear enunciation:
  8. Enunciating the phonemes clearly
  9. What about accents?

- Checking your subject knowledge
  10. How can phonological awareness develop into phonemic awareness?
  11. Developing basic blending and segmenting
  12. What to do if you are worried about your accent

Strategy: Developing phonological awareness

Long before they begin matching sounds to letters, learners develop *phonological awareness*: an ability to hear and discriminate between different sounds. This essential preparation for literacy development is a key feature of most phonics programmes, with early phases focusing on phonological awareness before learners are introduced to phonemes (letter sounds) and the graphemes (letters) which correspond to them.

Teachers use many activities to attune learners to sounds all around them, before introducing them, orally, to sounds in words. They move on to oral blending of sounds to make words, so that learners learn to associate names of people and things with their initial sounds and later their final and medial sounds.

1. What activities can you use to develop phonological awareness?

Simple activities to develop learners' ability to distinguish between sounds include:

Listening walks

Take learners for a walk around the school and ask them to listen carefully to different sounds. Record these and play them back in the classroom and ask learners to identify the sounds and say where they heard them. Make recordings of a range of sounds, including animals, bells, traffic and musical instruments, and produce picture cards and later word cards to accompany them. Display all the pictures as you play the sounds and ask learners to match sounds to pictures.

Sound sequences

Clap rhythms or the syllables in names for learners to repeat. You might clap learners' names, with one clap for each syllable, and ask learners to say if the claps could represent their names. You can also clap names of popular TV programmes or songs.

Sound boxes

Collect items which make a distinctive sound, such as marbles to rattle in a jar, triangles, maracas, tambourines and rattles. Make the sounds with the items as you put them into a box. Ensure the learners can't see the items in the box and ask them to listen as you make sounds by rattling, shaking, tapping etc, and then ask them to identify which item makes which noise. Invite learners to take turns at making the sounds and add to or change the items in the box as they become more familiar with them.

2. How do learners acquire sounds?

Learners' oral language abilities develop long before they learn to read and write. They learn to separate words from each other and to make different sounds for different words. At first they make vowel sounds and sounds which are made at the front of the mouth like *b*, *d*, *t*, *p* and *m*. They hear single consonant sounds before clusters and so may say 'pease' for *please* and 'pay' for *play*. They often miss out syllables or consonant sounds (eg 'nana' for *banana*), but for most learners these early 'problems' gradually disappear and they learn to sound phonemes accurately.

A Spot of Theory

Caroline Bowen, a speech and language pathologist, provided examples of different phonological processes and the age when they typically change to normal pronunciation (Bowen, 2011). These include:

Phonological process	Example	Gone by approximately...
Fronting	car = 'tar' ship = 'sip'	3;6
Consonant harmony	mine = 'mime' kittycat = 'tittytat'	3;9
Weak syllable deletion	elephant = 'efant' potato = 'tato' television = 'tevision' banana = 'nana'	4;0
Cluster reduction	spoon = 'poon' train = 'chain' clean = 'keen'	4;0

When the processes continue to be problematic, learners may receive support from a speech-language therapist.

Makita wanted to develop her Reception class's phonological awareness so she discussed strategies with colleagues. She found that she could use activities as part of classroom management; for example, when learners were moving from their chairs to the carpet she would say *'Everyone whose name begins with /b/ can come now'* or *'Everyone wearing a jumper which is the colour r—'*. She also used sound to gain attention, for example making a *sh-sh-sh-sh-sh* sound or clapping a sequence for the learners to repeat, or ringing a tiny bell.

Makita introduced an 'I Spy' game using the initial sounds of words rather than their letter names. She played other games such as picking an alliterative adjective for a learner's name and asking the class to decide whose adjective it could be: *'I'm looking for lovely /lll/'* (Lucy) or *'I'm looking for fabulous /fff/'* (Faisal) etc.

When she wanted to ensure everyone had the things they needed for a lesson, she would ask them to hold things up by saying the initial sounds for *pencil*, *ruler*, *book* etc.

Strategy: Identifying phonemes

3. What is a phoneme?

A phoneme is the minimum unit of sound. In English we have around 44 different phonemes and we have only 26 letters in our alphabet. That means that some of our phonemes have to be written using more than one letter. For example, to make the 'ch' sound at the beginning of *chip* we need to combine *c* and *h*, and to make the 'sh' sound at the end of *fish*, we combine *s* and *h*. When we use two letters to make one sound we call this a digraph. Digraphs are common in many languages, including French where *c* and *h* combine to make a 'shh' sound as in *champagne*, *parachute* and *charade*, and German where *c* and *h* combine to make a sound which we don't have in English, in words like *acht* and *ich* (see Day 3 for more information about digraphs).

4. How can you develop phonemic awareness?

As you saw earlier, before learners start to match letters to sounds they need to develop phonological awareness. As they begin to see letters and match them to sounds, you need to develop their *phonemic awareness*: an understanding that letters can be sounded as phonemes and can be put together to create words. One way of doing this is to make use of names, places and words in the environment. You can begin this by labelling things in your classroom, including learners' drawers, cupboards etc. You can also make displays of familiar items and people and label them. Simple requests to find a person or thing which begins with a certain sound can be accompanied by showing the grapheme which represents that sound. You can also use grapheme charts and grapheme cards so that learners regularly see how sounds can be written down.

Why don't we learn whole words or clusters of sounds? Why does synthetic phonics focus on individual sounds? Johnston and Watson (2007) analysed research on learning to read and conducted studies of learners in Clackmannanshire in Scotland. They looked at differences in progress between those taught using *analytic phonics* in which whole words, syllables and rhymes are learned before individual sounds, and those who learned using synthetic phonics which focuses initially on the sounds of individual letters.

A Spot of Theory

Johnston and Watson (2007) concluded:

- Studies have shown that contrary to the idea that learners first become aware of large units such as rhymes, and only later become aware of smaller units such as phonemes, preschool learners' phoneme awareness skills are as good as their rhyme skills.

- Learners' preschool phoneme awareness ability is associated with early literacy skills, eg a knowledge of letters of the alphabet and the ability to recognise environmental print such as the product names on sweet wrappers.

- Learners acquire phoneme awareness better in the context of letters and print compared to learning without this concrete support.

- Learners who are taught phoneme awareness using letters and print develop significantly better reading and spelling skills than those who do not.

(Johnston and Watson, 2007, p 22)

Hannah was focusing on the phonemes which match the letters *i, n, m* and *d* with a group of five learners who needed additional support with phonics. She decided to create an interactive phoneme spotting game in order to help them associate sounds and symbols with names of people and things. Hannah made some picture cards of animals and various items with which learners would be familiar and put these around the classroom on walls, window sills, tables etc. She then spent some time teaching the common grapheme-phoneme correspondences for *i, n, m* and *d* with the learners before giving each learner 12 cards, three for each letter, and some adhesive putty. She underlined the *d* (*d*) so that learners wouldn't confuse it with *p*. She asked them to find as many pictures as possible which had names with the phonemes in them. When they found one, they could stick a grapheme card on it.

Learners enjoyed the activity and although some copied what others had done, Hannah did not mind this as the objective was for them to match letters to sounds and they were learning from each other. She used the game regularly with other graphemes and devised a phoneme spotting activity around the early years area of the school for the whole class.

Phoneme spotting

Strategy: Identifying graphemes

5. What is a grapheme?

A grapheme is a phoneme written down. When a single grapheme represents a sound as in *cat*, *dog* and *pig*, each of which has three phonemes represented by three graphemes, we usually refer to this as a *graph*. As you saw earlier, two letters making one sound are called a *digraph* (*ch*, *sh*, *ph*, *ou*, *oi*, *ay* etc). Sometimes three letters combine to make one sound (*igh* in *high*, *tch* in *match*) and these are called *trigraphs*. English even has *quadgraphs* where four letters make one sound (*ough* in *though*, *augh* in *caught*) (see Day 3).

In systemic synthetic phonics (SSP) programmes, learners are introduced to graphemes gradually and usually begin by looking at common graphs which can be used to create lots of words. Many programmes begin with the six letters *s*, *a*, *t*, *p*, *i*, *n* (sometimes *s*, *a*, *t*, *p*, *i*, *m*).

6. How can you represent the 44 phonemes?

The approximately 44 phonemes in English can be represented in many different ways. The tables below show examples of some of the most common grapheme representations.

Vowel phonemes	Examples and alternative spellings	Vowel phonemes	Examples and alternative spellings
/a/	**a**t	/oo/	b**oo**k w**oul**d p**u**t
/e/	l**e**g h**ea**d	/ar/	**ar**t f**a**st (in some regions)
/i/	b**i**g tast**ed**	/ur/	t**ur**n f**ir** t**er**m h**ear**d w**or**m
/o/	d**o**g w**a**s	/or/	w**or**n fl**oor** w**ar**m h**au**l j**aw** f**a**ll
/u/	h**u**g l**o**ve	/er/	doct**or** blist**er**
/ai/	r**ai**n w**ay** m**a**te st**a**tion	/ow/	fr**ow**n ab**ou**t
/ee/	tw**ee**t b**ea**t th**ie**f th**e**se	/oi/	c**oi**n t**oy**
/igh/	fr**i**ed m**igh**t b**y** f**i**ne k**i**nd	/air/	p**air**s b**ear** sh**are**
/oa/	l**oa**d l**ow** b**o**ne **o**ld	/ear/	**ear** ch**eer** h**ere**
/oo/	s**oo**n gl**ue** f**ew** t**u**ne		

Consonant phonemes	Examples and alternative spellings	Consonant phonemes	Examples and alternative spellings
/b/	**b**ag	/s/	**s**un hou**se** **c**ity sin**ce**
/d/	**d**og	/t/	**t**op ca**t**
/f/	**f**at **ph**otogra**ph** lau**gh**	/v/	**v**an
/g/	**g**ate	/w/	**w**ait **wh**en
/h/	**h**ad	/y/	**y**es
/j/	fu**dge** **g**erm lar**ge**	/z/	**z**oo plea**se** a**s**
/k/	boo**k** li**ck** fi**x** s**ch**ool	/th/	**th**en
/l/	**l**ot	/th/	**th**ick
/m/	**m**an co**mb** ha**mm**er	/ch/	**ch**ip ma**tch**
/n/	**n**ow **kn**ife **gn**aw	/sh/	**sh**op mi**ss**ion **ch**ef
/p/	**p**ot ha**pp**y	/zh/	plea**s**ure
/r/	**r**at **wr**ong	/ng/	si**ng**

7. What are alternative graphemes?

A problem when learning phonics in English is that there are many variations in the graphemes you can use for most phonemes. In some languages, such as Finnish and Italian, there is much greater regularity, with the same grapheme representing each phoneme consistently. In English, there are examples such as those below where the phoneme can be represented in different ways.

The /k/ sound as in *kit* can be *c* in *cat*, *ck* in *sock*, *ch* in *school*, *cc* in *account* etc.

The /s/ sound in *sit* can be *c* in *city*, *ss* in *miss*, *c* in *race* etc.

For guidance on how you can support learners, see Day 4.

Ellie used a magnetic board with her Reception class to move graphemes around and create words. She made her own letter cards and put tiny magnets on the back of each and then modelled this working with the whole class. She began with *s, a, t, p* and found that most learners could help her to make words such as *at, sat, sap, pat* and even *past*. When someone suggested *as*, Ellie was careful to get learners to sound the 's' as it is sounded in *as* ('zz') and to tell them that sometimes in words like *as, has* and *was*, 's' is sounded a little differently.

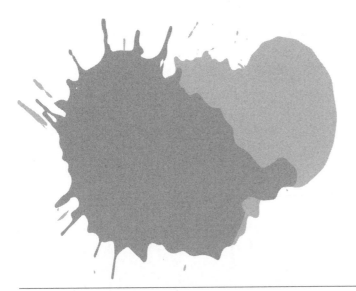

Over a five-week period, Ellie introduced sets of graphemes in the order suggested by *Letters and Sounds* (DfES, 2007):

Set 1	s	a	t	p	
Set 2	i	n	m	d	
Set 3	g	o	c	k	
Set 4	ck	e	u	r	
Set 5	h	b	f, ff	l, ll	ss

These 23 graphemes enabled the learners to make lots of words, including some which did not actually exist such as *tiss* and *rull*. When such a word was created, Ellie checked the dictionary before asking learners to decide what such things might be. She felt this was good practice for learners who would be taking the *Phonics Screening Check* the following year in which invented or *pseudo words* are used to check learners' phonemic awareness (see Day 2).

A Spot of Theory

Jolliffe et al (2015, p 22) suggest that teachers support learners in their selection of the correct grapheme in the following ways:

● *Teaching common rules for graphemes. If you take ai/ay as a common example, the general rule is that the ai grapheme appears in the middle of a word (as in sn**ai**l, p**ai**nt, r**ai**d), while the ay grapheme is used at the end (as in pl**ay**, Saturd**ay**, aw**ay**).*

● *Grouping words by grapheme type (as in night, light, sight, fright) to enable learners to learn several words by association and to understand common rules and spelling patterns.*

● *Ensuring the meaning of the word in question is clearly understood. A simple example of this is asking learners to spell or read the words see/sea.*

● *Revisiting common groups of words with grapheme variations to ensure that learners have regular reminders through a variety of games and activities.*

Strategy: The importance of clear enunciation

It is important that learners hear phonemes pronounced correctly; otherwise you may find learners' early writing includes 'words' such as *bt* (for *butter*), *cl* (for *colour*) and *sm* (for *summer*). These errors can occur when learners hear the letters being sounded with an additional sound, so that *s* sounds like 'suh' rather than 'sss', and *m* sounds like 'muh' instead of 'mmm'. Most teachers are aware of the importance of 'clean' enunciation without the added *schwa*, but sometimes well-meaning parents and carers may cause confusion by adding a schwa or even naming the letters by their 'sound', as in *Sam begins with a suh*. Sam will be more likely to learn how to spell his name if he hears it as */sss/a/mmm/* than *suh/a/muh*.

8. Enunciating the phonemes clearly

How can you avoid the schwa?

The schwa is the most common sound in English and can be heard in words such as *sof**a***, *doct**or***, *read**er***, *less**on*** and *th**e***. The schwa is not usually taught as a sound because it is thought that this might confuse learners. The schwa is also the sound we make when giving letter sounds incorrectly, for example, *b**uh***, *c**uh*** and *d**uh*** for *b*, *c* and *d*.

It is important that you practise sounding the consonants without the schwa and enunciate clearly when working with children. For most letters this is quite easy, but some letters are very difficult to sound without some additional sound. Try sounding the alphabet below:

a b c d e f g h i j k l m n o p q r s t u v w x y z

For some letters is quite easy to avoid making an additional sound:

a c e f h i j k l m n o r s u v w x y z

However, some sounds made at the front of the mouth (*b*, *d*, *p* and *t*) are more difficult and it is only really possible to try to reduce the extra sound to make it as minimal as possible.

Q is interesting as it is actually a single /k/ sound but is taught as *qu* (sounded 'kw') in some phonics programmes. This is understandable since in English words *q* is always followed by *u*, but this may cause confusion for some learners, especially as they may see names of countries (*Iraq* and *Qatar*) without a following *u*, and some companies deliberately misspell *quick* as *kwik*.

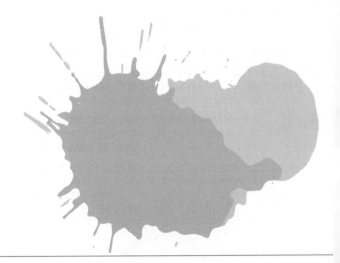

9. What about accents?

Accent refers to the way that words are pronounced. Some beginner teachers become concerned when their accents differ from those of the learners they teach. They worry that learners will not understand them and that this may be a problem when teaching phonics. Most phonics programmes give little attention to this issue, but there are situations where confusion can arise, for example when a teacher who pronounces words like *grass* and *bath* with a long /ar/ sound works with learners who use a short /a/ sound and vice versa.

The vowel phoneme used in *but* is often the same as that in *foot* in the north of England, and many northern speakers don't use the phoneme southern speakers use in *but* at all. Most variations in accents are associated with vowel sounds, but there are some variations in consonant sounds too. For example, in the Scouse accent associated with Merseyside, the /k/ sound in words like *chicken* can be sounded similarly to the way *ch* is sounded in German, for example in *ich bin*.

It is important, therefore, to remember that Standard English can be spoken with any accent and that the national curriculum does not require learners to speak with a particular accent. It does, however, state: *'Pupils should be taught to speak clearly and convey ideas confidently using Standard English'* (DfE, 2013, p 10).

A Spot of Theory

Crystal (2005, p 290) distinguishes between accent and dialect:

Accent refers just to distinctive pronunciation, whereas dialect refers to spoken grammar and vocabulary as well. The difference between bath with a 'short a' and bath with a 'long a' [a:] is to do with accent, as this is solely a matter of pronunciation. But if we heard one person say 'He done it' and another say 'He did it', we would refer to them as using different dialects, because a grammatical difference is involved. Similarly, the choice between wee bairn and small child is dialectical, because this is a contrast in vocabulary.

Checking your subject knowledge

10. How can phonological awareness develop into phonemic awareness?

Songs like 'Old MacDonald Had A Farm' work particularly well as they include animal noises. Talk with learners about the noises different animals make. Discuss different barks for different dogs and ask learners to make the sound their own pets make, as they sing. Modern foreign language learners could talk about the sounds they attribute to different animals, which may be different from the *wuffs*, *moos* and *baas* often used in Britain.

Song lyrics can be changed to include members of the class, familiar places and so on. They can also be adapted so that a well-known song is sung with some words only sung as an initial sound, for example:

Old MacDonald had a f---,

ee-ay-ee-ay-o,

And on that f he had some p---

ee-ay-ee-ay-o,

This can be developed later by writing the names down and completing them.

11. Developing basic blending and segmenting

Every word can be broken down or segmented into its individual sounds to help us to read. Look at the words below and decide how many sounds or phonemes each has:

sat   tin   pin   tint   stint

How did you do? *Sat* has three phonemes – /s/a/t/. *Tin* and *pin* also have three. *Tint* has four: /t/i/n/t/ and *stint* has five: /s/t/i/n/t. A common mistake is not to count the vowel sound as a phoneme and to think that *sat* is two phonemes – /sa/t. But if you change the vowel in the middle to an *i* or an *e* you can hear that one sound changes when we say *sit* or *set*.

Activity: making words from *s, a, t, p, i, n*

❋ Look at *s, a, t, p, i, n* and see how many words you can create using only those letters once each in each word. There are at least 34 possibilities (see opposite for some possible answers).

You could use grapheme cards, which are simply cards with individual graphemes written on them that can be moved around to make words.

12. What to do if you are worried about your accent

If you are concerned that your accent may be affecting your ability to teach phonics there are some possible solutions.

❋ Modify your accent when teaching phonics so that it is more like the learners'. This may seem a little drastic, but most people vary their accents in different situations – have you noticed how some people have a telephone voice, for instance?

❋ Talk about accents. There may be several different ones in your class so it might help if you told learners that some sounds and words are pronounced differently by different people. Learners watch television and are used to hearing a range of accents. Make this a topic for discussion.

- Be positive about accent variations. As long as people speak clearly and enunciate letters clearly, they can usually be understood.

- Encourage learners to use different accents sometimes, perhaps saying a word in a range of different ways.

Strategy in action

Demi's Year 2 class included learners from various parts of Britain and some for whom English was an additional language. Several new learners had joined the school recently as their parents had taken up posts at a newly opened prison nearby. With several different accents in the class, Demi felt she needed to teach phonics while not denigrating the way in which anyone spoke.

Demi made accents a topic for discussion and began by reading stories using different accents for each character. She omitted text which indicated who was speaking (*said Tony*, *called Eve* etc) and occasionally asked learners which character they thought had just spoken. In phonics lessons she helped learners sound words and then said the words in different accents, asking learners how each character from their story might say them. She emphasised that there was nothing "wrong" with any of the accents and that the important thing was that people who spoke with different accents could understand each other. Far from confusing the learners, Demi found that this approach helped them tune into phonemes better and to appreciate that some vowel phonemes, in particular, could be sounded in different ways by different people.

Reading stories can illustrate accents

Answers

You were asked to look at *s, a, t, p, i, n* and see how many words you can create using only those letters once each in each word. Here are some possibilities:

sat	spat	pin	sin	pit	pits
tin	pan	tan	tans	at	in
as	an	pint	pat	pats	past
pins	spin	sit	tap	taps	pans
pints	paint	paints	satin	nip	
nips	tip	tips	sip	pain	

Checklist

Use this to keep a record of what worked well for you and what didn't. A strategy that works with one learner or group of learners may not work so well with another. Keeping a checklist helps you to work out what factors or learner characteristics call for one approach rather than another. There's a line at the bottom for you to add your own most frequently used strategy, if it's not already included in the list.

Strategy	Tried it with…	On… (date)	It worked	It didn't work	Worth trying again?
1. What activities can you use to develop phonological awareness?					
2. How do learners acquire sounds?					
3. What is a phoneme?					
4. How can you develop phonemic awareness?					
5. What is a grapheme?					
6. How can you represent the 44 phonemes?					
7. What are alternative graphemes?					
8. Enunciating the phonemes clearly*					
9. What about accents?					
10. How can phonological awareness develop into phonemic awareness?					
11. Developing basic blending and segmenting					
12. What to do if you are worried about your accent					
Your own strategy?					

DAY 2: Decoding and encoding, blending and segmenting

Day 2 looks at the skills of decoding, encoding, blending and segmenting and how these can be developed through phonics teaching. It also explores, later in the chapter, the fact that these processes are reversible. It considers the role that decodable books and reading scheme books have to play in the development of reading skills.

You now know about phonemes and graphemes (see Day 1). As a reader and writer, once you are familiar with phonemes and graphemes you use these to read and spell. By decoding and encoding, blending and segmenting you use phonemes and graphemes to allow you to do this. Let's begin by defining what is meant by these terms:

Decoding is the recognition of symbols or letters and transferring them into sounds in order to read them. You read the grapheme and identify the phoneme that it represents in order to be able to understand what you are reading.

Encoding involves spelling and is the process of turning sounds into symbols or letters. You identify the phoneme and transfer it in to the grapheme that represents it in order to be able to spell it.

Blending is linked to decoding and enables us to read. Once you have decoded a phoneme, you blend it with others to read words.

Segmenting is linked to encoding and enables us to spell. You break a word into its separate graphemes and phonemes in order to be able to spell it.

The skills needed to read unfamiliar words are stipulated by the Department for Education (DfE). The national curriculum states that pupils in Year 1:

> ...need to develop the skill of blending the sounds into words for reading and establish the habit of applying this skill whenever they encounter new words. This will be supported by practice in reading books consistent with their developing phonic knowledge and skill and their knowledge of common exception words.
>
> (DfE, 2013, p 20)

Today's strategies

- Decoding and encoding:
    1. Finding out about decoding and encoding
    2. Phonemes stay the same but spellings change

- Blending and segmenting:
    3. Exploring blending and segmenting
    4. Supporting learners in Key Stage 2 with blending and segmenting

- CVC, VC, CV and CVCC words:
    5. Discovering CVC words
    6. What about CVCC words?
    7. Exploring other letter combinations

- Using blending and segmenting skills:
    8. Finding out if pseudo words are nonsense
    9. Checking out the *Phonics Screening Check*

- Using decodable texts:
    10. Decoding: the role of decodable texts
    11. Using 'real' books
    12. Multi-modal texts

Strategy: Decoding and encoding

1. Finding out about decoding and encoding

As discussed in the introduction, decoding means the reading of symbols or letters and transferring them into sounds to make words. Encoding involves spelling and is the process of turning sounds into symbols or letters. Decoding and encoding are the mechanisms by which phonics is applied to reading and writing. Learners should be taught to apply these processes when engaging with text through reading or writing.

The processes of decoding and encoding are reversible; the same word can be decoded to read it and then encoded to spell it, and vice-versa. It is crucial that we make this explicit when teaching by providing opportunities to both read and write graphemes for the corresponding phonemes during every phonics teaching session. This is often done through quick-fire activities, perhaps reading flashcards with words containing key phonemes, practising writing those words on whiteboards or engaging with those phonemes and words in sentences and texts. The popular phonics programmes (see Day 5) commonly used in schools have learning and practising of decoding and encoding as an integral part of the planning sequence.

Ensuring that opportunities are provided to decode and encode text provides valuable reinforcement of the grapheme-phoneme correspondences (GPCs). While these two processes are reversible, they require different skills. Decoding, or reading, requires recognition memory as the letters act as a prompt. For encoding, the visual prompt is not present and the learner must use recall memory, which is more difficult.

Let's practise decoding and encoding. Read the words in the table below and then separate them into their phonemes. It might be a good idea to work with a friend or colleague, so that you can sound the phonemes aloud and have a partner to check your answers. One has been done for you, and you'll find the answers on the opposite page.

✸ Count the number of phonemes after segmenting the words.

Word	Separate graphemes and phonemes	Number of phonemes
crash	/c/ /r/ /a/ /sh/	4
said		
mirror		
shampoo		
boiler		
stretch		
football		
shopping		

2. Phonemes stay the same but spellings change

English is a complex opaque spelling system, compared to many other languages. As a result of this, the English alphabetic code needs to be carefully taught to ensure that the 44 phonemes and their common spellings are taught fully and rigorously. As we have seen, phonemes stay the same but they can be represented by different graphemes. For example, the phoneme /ie/ can be written as 'igh' in *light* and 'i' in *tiger* or 'y' in *fly* or 'i–e' in *bike*. So, when decoding, learners need to be taught to choose between alternative graphemes in order to identify the phoneme and read the word.

Even though phonemes stay the same they will appear in words in different combinations, and it is decoding and encoding skills that will help a learner to unlock the alphabetic code and enable them to read and spell words in any form. Early readers will often use decoding and encoding skills to know the difference between words like *acts* and *cats*, and *angles* and *angels*.

Words are often modified by prefixes and suffixes, for example *build/rebuild* or *shop/shopping*, and decoding and encoding can be key to recognising the change (see Day 6). It is because of the complexity of the English language that learners will also need to be taught to use decoding and encoding skills to recognise, read and spell those words that don't contain regular GPCs. These are now often referred to as *common exception words* (see Day 4).

A Spot of Theory

Jolliffe et al (2015) note that in the past there has often been a focus on phonics for reading to support decoding the text without emphasising that alongside this learners should be taught to spell the words. The emphasis on reversibility helps reinforce learning, for you can always read words you can spell, but you cannot always spell words you can read.

Strategy in action

The teachers and learners in an urban primary school in Teesside often used the local environment to go on reading trails. They used road signs, shop names, logos, advertising hoardings etc to illustrate maps and diagrams drawn to record their journey. Adults helped the learners with the phonemes and graphemes that were unfamiliar to them. In annotating these maps, learners would be supported in using their decoding and encoding skills in meaningful situations.

Answers

Word	Segmented into phonemes	Number of phonemes
crash	/c/ /r/ /a/ /sh/	4
said	/s/ /ai/ /d/	3
mirror	/m/ /i/ /rr/ /or/	4
shampoo	/sh/ /a/ /m/ /p/ /oo/	5
boiler	/b/ /oi/ /l/ /er/	4
stretch	/s/ /t/ /r/ /e/ /tch/	5
football	/f/ /oo/ /t/ /b/ /a/ /ll/	6
shopping	/sh/ /o/ /pp/ /i/ /ng/	5

Strategy: Blending and segmenting

3. Exploring blending and segmenting

Blending and segmenting are closely linked to decoding and encoding. As mentioned in the introduction to this chapter, blending is linked to decoding and enables us to read. Once we have decoded a phoneme, we blend it with others to read words. Blending involves looking at a written word, looking at each grapheme and using knowledge of GPCs to work out which phoneme each grapheme represents and then merging these phonemes together to make a word. This is the basis of reading. Within synthetic phonics, blending is the prime strategy through which words are read.

Segmenting is linked to encoding and enables us to spell. We break a word down into its separate graphemes and phonemes in order to be able to spell it. Segmenting involves hearing a word, splitting it up into the phonemes that make it up, using knowledge of GPCs to work out which graphemes represent those phonemes, and then writing those graphemes down in the right order. This is the basis of spelling. Segmentation is the reverse of blending; it is the ability to split up a spoken word into phonemes.

As with decoding and encoding, blending and segmenting are reversible processes. Therefore, it is crucial that you make this explicit when teaching by providing opportunities to both read and write graphemes for the corresponding phonemes during every phonics teaching session. Again, as with decoding and encoding, the popular phonics programmes commonly used in schools have the learning and practising of decoding and encoding as an integral part of the planning sequence. You can find out more about planning for phonics, and phonics programmes, in Day 5.

A Spot of Theory

McGuinness (2004) explored the confusion between segmenting and blending, which leads to the assumption that reading involves blending and spelling involves segmenting, but that both are not linked. However, as McGuinness states, this is not what happens, and she gives the following example:

- Learners see an unfamiliar word, eg *sting*.

- To read it a learner sounds out each phoneme: /s/ /t/ /i/ /ng/. They blend it into a word and check the outcome. It is common for beginning readers to segment correctly and blend incorrectly: /s/ /t/ /i/ /ng/: and say 'sing'.

- To spell the word *sting*, the learners say the word, hear each segment in sequence and blend the segments into the word as they write.

(McGuinness, 2004, p 161)

In reality, segmenting and blending are connected in both reading and spelling. It is not the case that one relates to reading and the other to spelling. They are interrelated. For experienced readers the process happens at speed. You only become aware of this interplay when you encounter a word you cannot read or spell, as early readers do frequently.

4. Supporting learners in Key Stage 2 with blending and segmenting

It is important to revisit the alphabetic code, noting gaps in learners' knowledge, and supporting the practising of blending and segmenting, using the sounds learners are confident with. This will ensure they are eventually able to decode and encode more accurately and independently. It is a good idea to revisit these strategies in short sharp bursts throughout the day.

It may be beneficial to create word banks of decodable words, to support learners who struggle to blend, for all areas of the curriculum. Subject-specific word banks are useful when studying a particular topic. Support learners by placing dots and dashes to help them identify the separate phonemes, and then in turn blend and segment the words they will need. For example:

match　　　　*wood*

.. —　　　　　— .

If learners have previously seen a word, they are less likely to be anxious or worried by it.

You should identify and revise common exception words (see Day 4) that may arise in texts the learners are reading, so that they do not become frustrated. You might help learners identify words they might struggle to read before embarking on reading, and discuss the vocabulary they may find difficult.

It is important to use appropriate texts, and you should offer books that are designed to engage older learners. Learners should be encouraged to choose books that interest them. These may be more suitable than the reading schemes that have been developed to supplement phonics teaching and are designed for the younger reader. They can cover topics relevant to older readers' levels of maturity, while giving them confidence when using blending and segmenting skills.

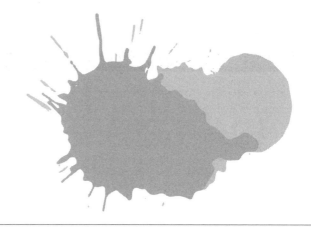

Strategy: CVC, VC, CV and CVCC words

5. Discovering CVC words

Blending and segmenting skills are introduced early in the teaching sequence and are initially used to spell a range of simple words. These are commonly known as consonant-vowel-consonant (CVC) words, and are some of the first words early readers will encounter. These words have three phonemes in the specific CVC order, for example *cat*, *bed*, *bit*, *hot* and *mud*. CVC words have three phonemes but not necessarily three sounds, as some CVC words have digraphs and trigraphs on them. Digraphs consist of two graphemes that represent one phoneme, for example the 'th' in *this*, 'sh' in *fish* and 'oa' in *boat*. Trigraphs have three graphemes that represent one phoneme, for example the 'igh' in *night* and the 'dge' in *hedge*. You can find out more about digraphs and trigraphs on Day 3. So, although CVC words only have three phonemes they might have more than three letters, and it is therefore best to teach learners about the numbers of sounds (phonemes) rather than the number of letters. Here are examples of CVC words with more than three letters:

Word	Consonant (C)	Vowel (V)	Consonant (C)
chip	ch	i	p
push	p	u	sh
heal	h	ea	l
when	wh	e	n
hoop	h	oo	p
chick	ch	i	ck
thatch	th	a	tch

6. What about CVCC words?

Again, in a similar way to CVC words, although CVCC words have four sounds they might have more than four letters (see Day 6). The two consonants that are side by side at the end of the word must not be a digraph that represents one phoneme, but must be two separate graphemes that represent two separate phonemes. These are known as adjacent consonant blends, and you can find out more about these on Day 3. This, therefore, reinforces the idea that teaching learners about the number of phonemes is most important. Here are some examples of CVCC words, some with four letters and some with more (the adjacent consonant blends are in bold):

Words	C	V	C	C
ha**lt**	h	a	l	t
ye**lp**	y	e	l	p
fir**st**	f	ir	s	t
chi**mp**	ch	i	m	p
gi**ft**	g	i	f	t
thir**st**	th	ir	s	t
bu**lk**	b	u	l	k
roa**st**	r	oa	s	t
pai**nt**	p	ai	n	t

7. Exploring other letter combinations

Learners should be taught VC words, such as *at, is, up* and *on*, early in the teaching sequence. They should also be taught CV words, such as *do, so* and *be*. Many of these CV words contain unusual GPCs, where one or more phonemes are represented by graphemes that don't follow the usual pattern. For example, in the word *do* the 'o' makes an /oo/ phoneme rather than the expected /o/. These are currently often referred to as *common exception words*, and we will discuss these on Day 4.

There are many other words with different letter combinations, such as CCVC and CCVCC, and you can find out more about these when we discuss spelling on Day 6.

In an Early Years Foundation Stage (EYFS) class, the teacher, Carolyn, had taught Phase 2 and some of Phase 3 of *Letters and Sounds* (DfES, 2007), where CVC words are introduced. She then provided the learners with their own mini books. On each page, the learners were first encouraged to write the CVC word *dog* or *cat*, followed by the CVC word *can*. They then selected a different word from a list that they could decode (eg *hop, pop, pat* etc):

    Dog can *hop*

    Dog can *pop*

    Dog can *pat*

    Dog can *tip*

    Dog can *nip*

    Dog can...

The learners were encouraged to share their books with a friend, act out the sentences and to provide an illustration. After being displayed in the reading corner for all to share, the books were then taken home to be shared with parents and carers and to be added to with other similar sentences. Some of the learners brought other versions of the books into school that they had made at home about a sibling, favourite pet or much-loved toy.

Using blending and segmenting skills

✸ Before you go on, let's check your understanding. Look at the words in the table below and decide whether they are VC, CV, CVC or CVCC words. Remember it's the number of sounds (phonemes) that are important, not the number of letters. The first one has been done for you, and you can find the answers at the end of the strategy.

Word	Type (VC, CV, CVC or CVCC)
which	CVC
do	
seal	
salt	
if	
chop	
chops	
me	
watch	

How did you get on? If you are new to phonics, being secure in your knowledge and understanding of types of words, and the blending and segmenting skills you use to read and spell them, can feel like it might take some time to master. This can also be the case for the learners you are teaching. One way of practising (and assessing) blending and segmenting skills is to use pseudo words.

8. Finding out if pseudo words are nonsense

Pseudo words, commonly known as nonsense words or 'made up' words, are often used in phonics teaching. They are used as an assessment tool in the *Phonics Screening Check*, details of which you can find in the next section. They are pronounceable combinations of letters that can be read by the application of GPC skills, but they are not real words in English. They rely on word recognition abilities without the need for comprehension or understanding of the meaning of a word. They are therefore thought of as a useful tool for developing phonic skills.

A Spot of Theory

Siegel (2008) completed some research that found that in a complex orthography such as English, the best measure of phonological processing skill is the reading of pseudo words. Pseudo words can be read by application of grapheme–phoneme conversion rules even though the words are not real and have not been encountered in print or in spoken language.

Daniel's class were delighted when he told them they were going to start 'talking nonsense'. In order to practise their blending and segmenting skills, and to enable Daniel to assess the learners' progress, the learners used large grapheme cards, containing those graphemes they were already familiar with, to make their own pseudo words. Daniel established some rules; the words must follow either a CVC or CVCC pattern and they must contain only known graphemes that the learners were confident with. As well as reading and spelling the words, the learners had great fun making up definitions for the words they had invented.

✹ How else might the learners in Daniel's class use the pseudo words they created?

9. Checking out the *Phonics Screening Check*

To assess learners' progress, a statutory *Phonics Screening Check* was introduced in 2012, to be administered to all learners in the summer term of Year 1. The purpose of the screening check is to assess whether learners have achieved the age-expected level of understanding of phonics and to identify learners who may be struggling in developing phonics skills.

The screening check contains 40 words, divided into two sections of 20 words each. Both of the sections contain a mixture of real and pseudo words. The pseudo words are designed to test learners' ability to read GPCs, without the benefit of word comprehension, and also to be able to blend these into whole units or words. Although the words are considered to be 'nonsense', they contain the regular GPCs that have been taught through phonics programmes. The pseudo words are introduced to learners as 'alien' words and there is a picture shown next to each of these words in the check to show an imaginary creature to clearly demarcate these. It is

common practice to make sure learners are familiar with pseudo words and how to blend the GPCs in them.

An adult, often the classteacher, administers the screening check with each learner, on an individual basis. The learner's response to each word is recorded on the mark sheet, denoting if correct or incorrect and any comments noted against incorrect answers; for example, if a learner read some sounds correctly but not all, or if a learner tried to give a real word instead of a pseudo word. Scores for the screening check can be compared to a benchmark pass score, released by the DfE once all screening checks nationally have been completed. If a learner doesn't reach the benchmark pass, they are expected to complete the screening check again the following year, in Year 2.

Answers

Word	Type (VC, CV, CVC or CVCC)
which	CVC
do	CV
seal	CVC
salt	CVCC
if	VC
chop	CVC
chops	CVCC
me	CV
watch	CVC

Using decodable texts

10. Decoding: the role of decodable texts

Decodable texts contain words that are at an appropriate phonic level for learners to decode. They contain known phonemes and often have short sentences, as a result of the limited vocabulary that can be used, especially in books designed for very early readers. As a result, they may also be limited in meaning and interest. The texts might contain common exception words that learners are already familiar with. They are the basis of many of the reading schemes that are popular in primary schools.

Decodable texts provide vital practice for learners in reading known phonemes and blending them into words. Learners who read decodable texts based on their phonic ability often demonstrate an enjoyment in reading as they can read without support from adults. While they should not be the only books learners are exposed to, they are often thought of as a good tool to encourage learners to read independently and with success. It is widely acknowledged that they should be used as part of a rich language curriculum and that learners should frequently be offered the opportunity to access other reading materials. Decoding and blending skills are not the only skills learners use when reading, and they are just one element of developing successful readers.

11. Using 'real' books

Although 'real' books (those that don't follow a decodable format and have words with phonemes and graphemes that are unfamiliar to learners) aren't necessarily immediately accessible to all readers, they are key to providing a rich reading environment. Learners can access texts with topics that interest them. They can read non-fiction books that provide them with the information they need. Hearing stories and sharing texts with an adult are a good way to begin to access 'real' books. When encouraging learners to read the books, teachers can take a prepared reading approach, highlighting and discussing unfamiliar words and discussing vocabulary before learners embark on reading. Reading the texts in small, manageable chunks or adult and learner taking turns to read are also often successful strategies.

A Spot of Theory

Solity and Vousden (2009) carried out an analysis of reading scheme texts and 'real' books that revealed that real books offered learners the same opportunities to develop sight vocabulary and phonic skills as the reading scheme texts. They concluded that as real books have 'the same structure and representation of core skills as reading schemes' their advantages greatly outweigh those of the reading scheme. For example, they argue that real books provide better opportunities for learners to 'map newly acquired phonic and sight vocabulary skills to texts' as well as offering more choice, which can have an impact on language acquisition and general knowledge.

(*cited in Levy, 2009*, p 365)

12. Multi-modal texts

Along with the real books versus scheme books discussion, there is now also a debate about paper books versus e-readers. Whereas many readers embrace technology and read books, newspapers etc on electronic devices, there are others who still enjoy the experience of reading a 'proper' book. Although books are still the primary medium through which learners learn to read in primary schools today, teachers must consider the use of other media.

Learners now read in many other ways, both at school and at home. Handheld devices, which are now common in schools, can be used by learners to read, to write their own texts and design books, and to use applications to play phonics games and activities. Lots of the things learners read are now accompanied by moving graphics and images, sound and music. This enhances the experience for many learners, resulting in higher levels of stimulation and engagement. These are options to be explored in the classroom, although, it should be argued, not at the expense of the traditional book.

Strategy in action

Matthew had a group of reluctant readers in his Year 2 class. He noticed that some of these learners were already becoming disengaged with the reading scheme books the school used. Matthew introduced other reading media to the classroom, including e-readers, tablets, newspapers, comics and magazines. Each learner had the opportunity to create their own book, based on a topic that interested them. They initially used the devices to design and create electronic versions of the books. But Matthew wanted to allow the learners to see the value of a traditional book, so the learners made a paper copy of the electronic book they had designed. They read their books to the learners in the EYFS class and then took them home to share with parents and carers.

> Which other multi-modal texts might you introduce to a primary classroom?

Many ways to read

Checklist

Use this to keep a record of what worked well for you and what didn't. A strategy that works with one learner or group of learners may not work so well with another. Keeping a checklist helps you to work out what factors or learner characteristics call for one approach rather than another. There's a line at the bottom for you to add your own most frequently used strategy, if it's not already included in the list.

Strategy	Tried it with...	On... (date)	It worked	It didn't work	Worth trying again?
1. Finding out about decoding and encoding					
2. Phonemes stay the same but spellings change					
3. Exploring blending and segmenting					
4. Supporting learners in Key Stage 2 with blending and segmenting					
5. CVC, VC, CV and CVCC words[*]					
6. What about CVCC words?					
7. Exploring other letter combinations					
8. Finding out if pseudo words are nonsense					
9. Checking out the *Phonics Screening Check*					
10. Decoding: the role of decodable texts					
11. Using 'real' books					
12. Multi-modal texts					
Your own strategy?					

DAY 3: Digraphs and larger grapheme units

It would be easy if, in English, one phoneme was always represented by one grapheme. However, English is a complex language and it is not consistent and transparent. Unfortunately, as there are only 26 letters to represent 44 or more sounds, this means that written English has to have an advanced code where, frequently, sounds are represented by more than one letter and letters represent more than one sound. The alphabetic code refers to the understanding that letters are used to represent the speech sounds of our language. When the letters of the alphabet are used alone, this is referred to as the basic code. However, we also often use graphemes in twos, and in groups of three and four, to represent the sounds in our language; this is referred to as the advanced alphabetic code.

So if more than one grapheme is sometimes used to represent a phoneme, it's important to become familiar with what is meant by a *digraph*. A digraph is 'two letters that make one sound', or in other words, one phoneme that is represented by two graphemes. For example, in the word *chip*, /ch/ is a digraph because the /ch/ makes one sound and you don't say the /c/ and /h/ separately (incidentally, the /i/ and /p/ in *chip* are sounded out separately so they are individual graphs, not a digraph). Likewise, the /sh/ in *fish*, /th/ in *without* and /oa/ in *road* are all digraphs.

Day 3 explores different types of digraphs and how to teach them. It looks at groups of two letters that are not, in fact, digraphs. It also looks at longer grapheme units; those phonemes that are represented by three or four graphemes.

* Consonant digraphs:
  1. Considering consonant digraphs and their common spellings
* Finding out about adjacent consonants:
  2. The difference between consonant digraphs and adjacent consonant blends
* Understanding other types of digraphs:
  3. Double consonant digraphs
  4. Split vowel digraphs
* Vowel phonemes:
  5. A quick look at short vowel phonemes
  6. Take it more slowly with long vowel phonemes
* More about long vowel phonemes
  7. Checking long vowel phonemes
* Larger grapheme units:
  8. Let's try trigraphs
  9. And now for quadgraphs

Strategy: Consonant digraphs

1. Considering consonant digraphs and their common spellings

As discussed in the introduction, digraphs are two graphemes that represent one phoneme. And so, a consonant digraph is two consonants that represent one phoneme, for example /wh/ in *what*, /kn/ in *know* and /ph/ in *graph*. Sometimes these sounds have been referred to as having 'silent' letters; however, it is more accurate to teach learners that it is the two letters together that make one sound.

The grapheme-phoneme correspondences (GPCs) /sh/, /ch/, /th/ and /wh/ are usually taught first, as they are the most commonly occurring consonant digraphs in words that early readers encounter. As a result of this, the popular phonics programmes, some of which are explored in Day 5, introduce these early in the teaching sequence. Teaching using a clearly defined sequence will also be explored in Day 5. Younger learners often learn these GPCs first as either initial or final phonemes, perhaps /sh/ in *fish* and *shop*, and /ch/ in *much* and *chip*. You can refer back to Day 1 for more discussion about early readers.

Here are the most commonly taught digraphs and some examples of how they are used in common spellings:

Consonant digraph	Common spellings
ph	phone, graph
mb	thumb, numb
kn	knot, knock
wr	write, wring
sh	fish, shampoo
th	thin, wealth
ck	wreck, back
ch	chips, chemist
wh	whole, white
ng	ring, playing
nk	think, blank

A Spot of Theory

Debbie Hepplewhite, in her Simple to Complex Alphabetic Code Overview *(2007), notes that the way that the /ng/ phoneme is pronounced can be affected by accent, with some accents pronouncing it as two separate phonemes /n/ and /g/. She also states that the 'nk' grapheme is usually thought of as two separate sounds; however, some phonics programmes, such as* Read, Write, Inc., *teach it as a consonant digraph, making one sound, for reading and spelling.*

As you now know, phonemes can be represented by more than one grapheme combination; for example, the /ee/ phoneme can be represented by 'ee' as in *feel*, 'ea' as in *heat* and 'e' as in *me*. This is also the case with some consonant digraphs. There are some more complex and less common digraphs that learners will need to know, and might go on to learn, once they have mastered the commonly occurring consonant digraphs. They are sometimes thought of as alternative consonant digraphs; those that are not commonly used to make a recognised phoneme.

Here are the more complex consonant digraphs with some examples of how they are used in spellings:

Consonant digraph	Spellings
sc	science, scene
st	castle, bustle
ps	psyche, psalm
gn	gnat, gnaw
rh	rhyme, rhapsody
mn	hymn, autumn
gh	ghost, rough

In both of the tables in this strategy you will see that the consonant digraphs will often be found in certain parts of words, and these can be taught as common rules when learners are making choices about which graphemes to use in spellings. For example, the graphemes 'wr', 'gn' and 'wh' are most commonly found at the beginning of a word, whereas the graphemes 'mn', 'ck' and 'mb' are rarely or never found at the beginning as the initial phoneme. There are of course, as ever, exceptions to the rules; think of 'mn' as the beginning of the word *mnemonics*, for example.

You might have also noticed in the tables that some of the consonant digraphs can be used to represent more than one phoneme, and they can be sounded in different ways. Some examples of this include the 'ch' grapheme; it can make the /ch/ sound in *chief*, the /k/ sound in *school* and the /sh/ sound in *chef*. And what about 'gh'; it can make the /g/ sound in *ghost* and the /f/ sound in *rough*. It is worth noting that 'th' can make a voiced sound (from the back of the throat) in *that* and an unvoiced sound (from the tongue) in *bath*. Voiced sounds are made when the vocal cords vibrate, while voiceless sounds are made without vocal cord vibration.

Strategy: Finding out about adjacent consonants

2. The difference between consonant digraphs and adjacent consonant blends

Not all spelling patterns that have two consonants together are digraphs, and often consonants that are side by side actually represent more than one phoneme. For example, in the word *crab*, the two consonant graphemes /c/ and /r/, represent separate phonemes, so the word is segmented as /c/ /r/ /a/ /b/. It is the same in the words *dart*, *slip* and *brim*. These consonants that are side by side, but represent different phonemes, are commonly known as adjacent consonant blends. On Day 6 you can find out more about learning to spell words with adjacent consonants.

● Look at the letter patterns with double graphemes below. Check that you know which ones are digraphs and which ones are adjacent consonant blends. You can find the answers at the end of the strategy.

ch	br	wh	fl	sl
ph	kn	gr	th	wr
ng	sh	pl	ck	cr

Strategy in action

Ben's group of EYFS learners had been learning consonant digraphs for a term, and were already familiar with the four most common ones /sh/, /ch/, /th/ and /wh/. They were confident in recognising them and blending them, and could use them with some accuracy when writing. However, now that they were becoming familiar with the fact that a phoneme could be represented by two graphemes together, they were finding it difficult to distinguish between digraphs and adjacent consonant blends. Ben introduced mirrors into his phonics lessons. He modelled what he wanted the learners to do with the mirrors, and showed them how to make the shape of their mouths overly pronounced when sounding out letters; then they began to have a turn at doing this. This fascinated the learners, as they could watch their mouths moving, and knew that if their lips moved when sounding out both consonants that they were adjacent consonants that made more than one sound. They learned that if their lips stayed the same shape, and did not move to another shape when sounding out both consonants, that they were likely to be consonant digraphs that represented one phoneme.

● How might Ben move the learners away from using mirrors when learning consonant digraphs?

Digraph friends

Answers

The consonant digraphs are shaded.

ch	br	wh	fl	sl
ph	kn	gr	th	wr
ng	sh	pl	ck	cr

Strategy: Understanding other types of digraphs

3. Double consonant digraphs

When two matching consonants appear together, commonly referred to as 'double letters', they should be sounded as one sound, therefore, they are consonant digraphs. They usually make the same sound as their single letter counterparts, and so 'ss' makes the /s/ phoneme, 'mm' makes the /m/ phoneme and 'zz' make the /z/ phoneme. The double consonant digraphs indicate to the reader that the preceding vowel should be sounded with a 'short' sound. The short vowel sounds relate to the sounds in *mass*, *better*, *winner*, *horror* and *buzzed* denoted as: /a/, /e/, /i/, /o/, /u/, respectively, and said in a quick, 'staccato' manner. You can find out more about the short vowel phonemes in Strategy 5.

The table opposite shows the double consonant digraphs and some examples of how they are used in common spellings.

As with the other consonant digraphs already discussed, there are common rules that we can teach learners when choosing to use double consonant digraphs or not. For example, a double consonant digraph is often used before a word is modified by a suffix, eg *grab/grabbed* and *rip/ripping*. Also, double consonant digraphs are not usually found at the beginning of a word, and so children can be taught that the sensible option is to choose the single grapheme representation of a phoneme in the initial position of a word. As ever you must be mindful of exceptions; the double 'll' grapheme is commonly used in names, such as *Lloyd* and *Llewellyn*, and Welsh place names, such as *Llandaff* and *Llandudno*. And let's not forget the friendly *llama*.

Double consonant digraph	Common spellings
bb	rubble, blubber
cc	accuse, accommodate
dd	ladder, middle
ff	gruff, differ
gg	digger, giggle
ll	miller, yelled
mm	summer, trimmed
nn	dinner, spinning
pp	whipped, slipper
rr	stirring, mirror
ss	hiss, scissors
tt	butter, hitting
zz	buzz, fizzing

A Spot of Theory

What is a diphthong?

The Oxford English Dictionary *(2010) tells us that a diphthong is:*

A sound formed by the combination of two vowels in a single syllable, in which the sound begins as one vowel and moves towards another.

Examples include oil, loud *and* Chloe. *A dipthong is not a traditional digraph in the sense that it represents one phoneme; however, it is one phoneme that morphs into another without the sounds being two fully formed independent sounds.*

4. Split vowel digraphs

Split vowel digraphs are a type of digraph that is a combination of two vowels, split by a consonant in the middle. The two vowels make one sound. The second of the vowels is an 'e'. The 'e' modifies the first vowel and alerts the reader that the first vowel should be pronounced with a long sound. We discuss long vowels sounds further in the next strategy. Split digraphs have often been called the 'magic e', because the 'e' magically transforms the sound of the other vowel. The split digraphs are 'a–e' as in *cake*, 'e-e' as in *mere*, 'i-e' as in *fire*, 'o–e' as in *lone* and 'u–e' as in *rule*. Usually if a suffix is added to modify a word, the 'e' is removed before the ending is added; however, the first vowel is still pronounced with a long sound, eg *like/liking* and *bake/baked*.

When introducing the split digraph in the autumn term of Year 1, Jacinta noticed that some of the learners in her phonics group were struggling to identify it in the words they were reading. As a consequence, the learners were not sounding out the phoneme with the appropriate long vowel sound, but with the short vowel sound with which they were most familiar. Jacinta introduced the group to a learning concept called the *Split Digraph Buddies*, a mischievous pair of vowels who were so naughty that they were not allowed to sit together without a consonant between them. However, these *Split Digraph Buddies* were such good friends that they held hands behind the consonant and still helped each other say the long vowel sound. Jacinta's group acted as the buddies, using large grapheme cards to illustrate the vowels and middle consonant. They drew their own 'buddies' on which to write the vowels and consonants and demonstrated the splitting and holding hands. By providing context and a chance to experience the concept, Jacinta was able to teach the group to recognise and read split digraphs more successfully.

❋ **What other strategies might be useful when teaching split digraphs?**

Strategy: Vowel phonemes

5. A quick look at short vowel phonemes

English has around 24 consonant sounds and 20 vowel sounds. Five of the vowel sounds are short vowel sounds. These are /a/, /e/, /i/, /o/, /u/. When you pronounce them they do not say their 'name'; in other words, they make the short sound /a/ as in *ant* rather than the long /ae/ as in *play* (let's look at long vowel phonemes next). As mentioned in the previous strategy, you say them with a 'staccato' voice. Short vowels usually sound like this:

/a/ as in *apple*

/e/ as in *egg*

/i/ as in *insect*

/o/ as in *bog*

/u/ as in *tug*

They appear in the words early readers are expected to access, such as CVC and CCVC words. As a result, the popular phonics programmes, some of which are explored in Day 5, introduce the short vowel phonemes early in the teaching sequence.

6. Take it more slowly with long vowel phonemes

So, English has around 24 consonant sounds and 20 vowel sounds. Besides the five short vowel sounds /a/, /e/, /i/, /o/, /u/ that we have already discussed above, there are 14 long vowel phonemes, shown in the adjacent table (Jolliffe et al, 2015, p 57):

Phonemes	Grapheme(s)	Common spellings
/ae/	ay, a–e, ai, a	play, take, snail, baby
/ee/	ee, ea, e	feel, heat, me
/ie/	ie, igh, y, i-e, i	tie, fight, my, bike, tiger
/oe/	oa, ow, o-e, o	float, slow, stone, nose
/u/	oo, ou, u	took, could, put
/ue/	oo, ue, ew, u-e	room, clue, grew, tune
/ow/	ow, ou	cow, loud
/oi/	oi, oy	coin, boy
/ur/	u, ir, er, ear, or	fur, girl, term, heard, work
/au/	au, or, oor, ar, aw, a	sauce, horn, door, warn, claw, ball
/ar/	ar, a	car, fast (regional)
/air/	air, ear, are	hair, bear, share
/ear/	ear, ere, eer	ear, here, deer
/ure/	ure, our	sure, tour
/ə/ (schwa)	er, ar, or, a	teacher, collar, doctor, about

If you have looked closely you'll see there are actually 15 long vowel phonemes in the table. The extra vowel sound is the *schwa* phoneme /ə/. This completes the 20 vowel sounds in total. The schwa is an unstressed vowel sound which is close to the phoneme /u/ (see Day 1). There are various spellings of this phoneme, including preach**er**, doll**ar**, fact**or**, th**e**, **a**lone. The schwa is said to be the most common sound in the language. It is sometime mistakenly added to pure sounds when phonemes are enunciated incorrectly. For example, if the phoneme /m/ is pronounced as 'muh' rather than 'mmmm', or the phoneme /r/ is pronounced as 'ruh' rather than 'rrrrrrr', then we can say that the schwa has been mistakenly added to the pure phoneme.

Long vowel phonemes usually contain digraphs, for example /ue/ written as 'oo' or 'ew' in *moon* and *flew*, or trigraphs, which are three letters that make one sound, for example /ear/ written as 'ere' and 'eer' in h**ere** or d**eer**. You can find out more about trigraphs in the next strategy. Occasionally, long vowel phonemes are represented by a single letter 'y', as in *try*, *fry*, *by* and *sty*; a single 'e' as in *me*, *be*, *he* and *she*; a single 'o' as in *go*, *so* and *no*; or a single 'a' as in *ma* and *pa*.

A person's accent can have an effect upon the way long vowel sounds are enunciated (see Day 1). Long vowel sounds can differ in different parts of the country. People from Newcastle, East Yorkshire, the Midlands, London, and the West Country, who have regional accents, often pronounce words like *hope*, *pain*, *book* and *state* differently, and it's usually the long vowel phoneme that changes in sound. This is worth considering when the person teaching has an accent that differs from the learners they teach.

A Spot of Theory

Snell and Andrews (2016) found that, when considering accent, the role of the teacher is to help learners understand the relationship between standard orthography (the conventional spelling system) and their own accent of English. The learners themselves can assist in this process.

When it comes to spelling, Kress (2000) makes the point that learners are highly skilled at recording accurately and precisely what they have actually heard, and thus their spellings can be taken as accurate data on the variety of English spoken in a particular area. In helping learners to move towards 'correct' spelling, Kress argues that teachers should first take account of the 'accurate' spellings learners produce. This will help teachers to understand learners' thinking/logic, and also recognises/rewards learners' abilities in recording speech.

Strategy: More about long vowel phonemes

7. Checking long vowel phonemes

This would be a good point to check your understanding of long vowel phonemes.

⭐ Look at the list of words below and see if you can identify those that contain long vowel phonemes. You can find the answers at the end of the strategy.

train	hoop	swim
play	frog	law
boy	house	fern

Teaching and learning long vowel phonemes can be challenging, perhaps because there are alternative spellings for each phoneme. For example, as we've seen in the table above, the phoneme /ur/ can be written in the following ways:

u – as in **fur**

ir – as in **girl**

er – as in **term**

ear – as in **heard**

or – as in **work**

⭐ What do you already know about the alternative spellings for long vowel phonemes?

⭐ How many ways can you find to spell the phoneme /ee/ as in *green*? There are at least nine ways, and you'll find some suggestions in the answers section at the end of the strategy.

Considering all the complexities, it seems like a daunting task to teach this to young learners. However, if it is done in lively, interactive and multi-sensory ways then learners should grasp the concept with success.

It is worth remembering, and worth teaching learners, that vowel phonemes are often found in certain places in a word, and that there are some general rules that can be used as a guide (with the proviso that there are usually exceptions to the rule!). Some vowel phonemes are not usually found at the end of a word. For example, the digraph 'ai' is virtually never used at the end of English words while 'ay' is usually used for the sound at the end of words and at the end of syllables. This is also true of the phoneme /au/; it is rarely found at the end of a word, where 'or' might be used instead (see Day 6).

Strategy in action

Suzie taught in a large, urban primary school in the North West of England. She found that her group of Year 1 learners, who were not making expected progress in phonics, and who required some additional intervention lessons to supplement their core phonics teaching, were struggling to remember the long vowel phonemes that were being introduced. Suzie felt that this was compounded by the fact that she was originally from Bristol, and spoke with a different accent to the learners. She experimented with adding actions to each vowel phoneme as she introduced them in her teaching. Suzie devised some of the actions herself, then once the learners felt confident, they began to devise their own to teach the other learners in their group. This meant that they were fully engaged in their learning, and it was personalised and very meaningful.

The popular phonics programme *Jolly Phonics*, as discussed on Day 5, uses actions to learn and remember the 44 phonemes. Here are the actions for a few of the vowel phonemes:

/ou/ Pretend your finger is a needle and prick your thumb saying 'ou, ou, ou'.

/oi/ Cup hands around your mouth and shout to another boat saying 'oi! Ship ahoy!'

/ue/ Point to people around you and say 'you, you, you'.

/er/ Roll hands over each other like a mixer and say 'er er er'.

/ar/ Open mouth wide and say 'ah'.

✸ Now have a go at making actions to match the vowel phonemes /ow/, /au/ and /ee/.

Answers

The long vowel phonemes commonly contain digraphs (two letters making one sound), eg /ae/ written as *ai* or *ay* or trigraphs (three letters making one sound), eg /air/ in h**air** or b**ear**.

The following words from the activity contain long vowel phonemes:

train – /t/ /r/ /**ai**/ /n/	*hoop* – /h/ /**oo**/ / p/
play – /p/ /l/ /**ay**/	*law* –/ l/ /**aw**/
boy – /b/ /**oy**/	*house* – / h/ /**ou**/ /se/
fern – /f/ /**er**/ /n/	

The phoneme /ee/ (as in *green*) can be spelled in at least nine ways, for example: *ea* (*mean*), *e* (*be*), *ie* (*siege*), *ei* (*deceive*), *e–e* (*serene*), *ey* (*key*), *y* (*folly*), *i* (*radio*), *i–e* (*marine*). Most of these spellings are uncommon and it is important to focus first on the most common spellings when teaching GPCs.

Strategy: Larger grapheme units

You now know graphs are single letters that represent one phoneme and digraphs are two graphemes that make one sound. There are larger groups of graphemes, common in many words, which represent a single phoneme.

8. Let's try trigraphs

Trigraphs are three graphemes that represent one phoneme, such as 'igh' in *night* and 'tch' in *watch*. They are usually a combination of vowels and consonants.

The GPCs /igh/ and /tch/ are usually taught first, as they are the most commonly occurring trigraphs in words that early readers encounter. As a result of this, the popular phonics programmes (see Day 5) introduce these relatively early in the teaching sequence.

Here are the most commonly taught trigraphs and some examples of how they are used in common spellings:

Trigraph	Common spellings
igh	high, fright
tch	catch, stitch
dge	hedge, ledger
oor	door, floor
ore	more, snore
air	hair, stairs
are	care, share
ire	fire, hire
ear	bear, hear
ure	sure, pure

As you now already know, phonemes can be represented by more than one grapheme combination, for example the /ee/ phoneme can be represented by 'ee' as in *feel*, 'ea' as in *heat* and 'e' as in *me*. This is also the case with some trigraphs. There are some more complex and less common trigraphs that learners will need to know, and might go on to learn, once they have mastered the more commonly occurring trigraphs.

A Spot of Theory

Jolliffe et al (2015) assert that if the English language had a consistent and transparent code, every sound would have just one letter assigned to it and it would be very simple to decode. As we only have 26 letters to represent 44 or more sounds, this means that written English has an advanced code where, frequently, sounds are represented by more than one letter, and letters represent more than one sound.

Here are the more complex trigraphs with some examples of how they are used in spellings.

Trigraph	Spellings
que	queue, plaque
gue	rogue, tongue
oar	soar, oars
our	four, colour
oul	could, should
ere	here, there
eau	plateau, bureau
eer	cheer, auctioneer
ier	pier, glacier
ssi	mission, aggression

In both of the tables you will see that the trigraphs will often be found in certain parts of words, and these can be taught as common rules when learners are making choices about which trigraphs to use in spellings. For example, the graphemes 'tch', 'dge' and 'ure' are most commonly found at the end of a word without a suffix, whereas the graphemes 'oul' (as in *would*) and 'ssi' (as in *mission*) are rarely found at the end as the final phoneme.

You might have also noticed that some of the trigraphs can be used to represent more than one phoneme, and they can be sounded in different ways. An example of this is the 'ear' grapheme; it can make the /air/ sound in *bear*, the /eer/ sound in *hear* and the /er/ sound in *earth*.

9. And now for quadgraphs

You will have probably deduced by now that quadgraphs are four graphemes that represent one phoneme, such as the 'ture' in *adventure*. They have both vowels and consonants combined. These are less common in the English language. Learners might go on to learn these once they have mastered digraphs and trigraphs.

Here are the quadgraphs and some examples of how they are used in common spellings:

Quadgraph	Common spellings
ough	rough, thought
eigh	sleigh, eight
augh	daughter
ture	aperture

As with the other grapheme units we have discussed, the quadgraphs can be used to represent more than one phoneme, and they can be sounded in different ways. An example of this is the 'ough' grapheme; it can make the /u/ sound in *borough*, the /oa/ sound in *dough*, the /or/ sound in *bought*, the /oo/ sound in *through* and the /ou/ sound in *plough*.

Strategy in action

Patel, a second-year undergraduate, was completing a teaching placement in a Year 2 class. Most of the class were progressing well in phonics and becoming independent in their reading. The learners were beginning to encounter a variety of words, with trigraphs, and occasionally quadgraphs, in their reading. They were feeling less confident about tackling more challenging words, so Patel decided to celebrate these words with more complex grapheme units. He dedicated a space in the classroom where they could post the trigraphs and quadgraphs they had found when reading. It often became a good-natured competition, with learners searching at home and in their local environment for appropriate words. Patel and the learners read and discussed the words together, using appropriate phonic strategies to effectively decode the words.

If you only try one thing from this chapter, try this*

Strategy	Tried it with...	On... (date)	It worked	It didn't work	Worth trying again?
1. Considering consonant digraphs and their common spellings					
2. The difference between consonant digraphs and adjacent consonant blends*					
3. Double consonant digraphs					
4. Split digraphs					
5. A quick look at short vowel phonemes					
6. Take it more slowly with long vowel phonemes					
7. Checking long vowel phonemes					
8. Let's try trigraphs					
9. And now for quadgraphs					
Your own strategy?					

DAY 4: Common exception words

First, you need to be clear what *common exception words* are. You will probably already be teaching them, but you may be using other terms for them.

Look at the words below and decide what they all have in common:

he   there   by   one   said

Did you notice that some of the letters don't sound the way we would usually expect them to – that they all contain an unusual grapheme–phoneme correspondence (GPC)? In the word *by*, the 'y' grapheme sounds like the letter 'i', in *said* the 'ai' grapheme sounds like the 'e' in *bed*, and so on. We often refer to these as 'tricky bits'. They are present in words that are not immediately accessible to early readers using phonemic strategies, such as saying the letter sounds and blending them together to read the word.

They are all *common exception words*, a term introduced in primary teaching in the national curriculum programme of study for English (2013). These words are defined by the DfE as common words containing unusual GPCs. It is a statutory requirement that pupils *'read common exception words, noting unusual correspondences between spelling and sound and where these occur'* (DfE, 2013, p 10). The suggested lists of common exception words that are included in the national curriculum programme of study for English (2013) are not exclusive, and learners should be taught many other words with unusual GPCs that are commonly used in the classroom and in popular phonics programmes such as *Letters and Sounds* and *Read Write Inc*.

Common exception words are often thought of as the most difficult to teach, because they have bits that don't follow regular spelling patterns, and unusual GPCs learners may never have come across before. This chapter shows you that this doesn't need to be the case and that although English is a complex language, with lots of words that don't seem to fit neatly with any others, there are many strategies for successfully teaching learners to read and spell common exception words.

Today's strategies

● Developing subject knowledge:
  1. Is the whole word tricky?
  2. Will these words always be tricky?

● Understanding how words work:
  3. Etymology matters
  4. Discussing morphology

● Reassessing opinions – it's not as hard as you think:
  5. Creating mnemonics
  6. Spelling tests with a twist
  7. Let's celebrate!

● Teaching techniques – it's really not that tricky:
  8. Using the most common 100 words

● More teaching techniques:
  9. Grouping words in other ways
  10. Exploring homophones
  11. Investigating heteronyms

Strategy: Developing subject knowledge

English is a complex language and is different from many other alphabetic languages. This is due to the complexity of syllable structure and inconsistent spelling systems (Wyse and Goswami, 2008). The nature of the English language means that the notion of 'one letter makes one sound' cannot be relied upon as it can in some other languages such as Italian and Finnish. In English, one grapheme can represent more than one phoneme, and one phoneme can be represented by several graphemes. In English, there are 44 phonemes, but more than 400 graphemes to represent them. As we've already seen, sometimes these graphemes are unusual when matched to the phoneme they represent. In contrast, it is interesting to consider that in countries such as Greece, Finland, Italy and Spain syllable structure is simple in words and there is usually a one-to-one correspondence between phonemes and graphemes. Words in these languages are often longer than words in English, but they are easier to segment into phonemes.

A Spot of Theory

Seymour et al (2003) suggest that English is exceptionally inconsistent in both reading and spelling, and that this inconsistency inhibits the rapid acquisition of grapheme–phoneme recoding skills.

However, as Crystal (2005) points out, there are only around 400 irregular spellings in the English language, and 84 per cent of words conform to a general pattern.

1. Is the whole word tricky?

Usually not all of each common exception word is tricky – they only have tricky parts. For example, in *said* the 'ai' grapheme is uncommon, because it sounds like the 'e' in *bed*. However, the 's' and 'd' sound the way we would expect them to, and so are not tricky at all, once we have mastered common phonemes. It is important to remember the words themselves are not tricky, but that they contain parts that are.

Very few words have more than one tricky part once learners have mastered basic GPCs. They can be shown groups of common exception words with common features so that they can focus on tricky parts and see that they can occur frequently; for example, once learners have learned *could*, they can also learn *should* and *would*.

2. Will these words always be tricky?

Some common words will always be thought of as 'tricky', because they contain GPCs that are uncommon in the English language. Take, for example, *shoe*; it is unusual for the 'oe' grapheme to sound like the 'oo' in *moon*. However, many of the common exception words that appear in the list of common exception words for Year 1 and 2 in the national curriculum programme of study for English (2013) will only be 'tricky' for a short time, as they have GPCs that have not yet been taught. For example, *by* and *my* are considered to be common exception words at Year 1, because learners have not yet been taught that 'y' can sound like the letter 'i', especially at the end of a short word. However, in Year 2, pupils are taught this spelling convention, and so *by* and *my* are no longer common exceptions, and can be learned alongside other words like *try*, *fry* and *dry*.

Nadia decided to focus on learners' names to discuss grapheme–phoneme variations with her Year 2 class. The class had recently written a story together, with Nadia as the scribe, and it had emerged that learners were unaware that some people with the same sounding names spelled them differently. Nadia focused on three names which were duplicated in the class but had different spellings: *Jayden* and *Jaden*; *Aiden* and *Aidan*; and *Stephen* and *Steven*. She asked the learners to say the names with her and then to look at them carefully and focus on the graphemes that differed.

Nadia emphasised that in each case the spelling was correct, but that many names could be spelled in different ways. The learners went on to look at other words that included the graphemes and at more examples of names which could be spelled in different ways, including *Katherine*, *Claire*, *John*, *Ashley* and *Mohammed*.

Which other groups of words, other than names, might Nadia use?

Strategy: Understanding how words work

3. Etymology matters

English words derive mainly from German, French and Greek, as well as from Latin and a range of other languages, but the spellings have evolved over the years in many ways. Crystal (2005) sums up the nature of the English language – it is derived from over 350 other languages and constantly acquires new words, both from other languages and from English speakers who create them. The *Oxford English Dictionary* includes new words every year, with recent entries including *jeggings*, *selfie* and *photobombing*. In 2016 the word of the year was *post-truth*. These influences leave us with a rich vocabulary. However, they also provide us with lots of inconsistencies in spelling, pronunciation and meaning.

In the above paragraph, we've actually been discussing the etymology of words in the English language. *Etymology* is the origins of words, and the ways they have developed over time. This can go some way to explaining why the English language has so many words with unusual GPCs. By teaching learners about the etymology of words, they can develop a better understanding of how words work in the English language, and that there are many exceptions to common rules.

4. Discussing morphology

Morphology is the way words are formed and structured, and their relationship with other words in the English language. There are common affixes (prefixes and suffixes) which can be added to words to modify their meanings. These can range from adding an *s* to *cat* or *-es* to *watch* to make them plural, to putting a prefix such as *re–* before a verb to make it mean that the action was performed again (*replay*, *reappointed*). These affixes can also be called morphemes – minimal units of meaning. So the word *replay* has two morphemes: *re–* and *play*, while *reappointed* has three: *re–*, *appoint* and *-ed*. The morphemes *play* and *appoint* have meaning by themselves and are called free morphemes, but *re–* and *-ed* cannot stand alone as words and only have meaning when added or bound to a free morpheme. They are known as bound morphemes.

Ahmed wanted to look at morphemes with his Year 4 class and chose the following:

unlikely	*disappear*	*trigraph*
supermarket	*minibeast*	*antifreeze* *wonderfully*

He explained that the words could be separated into units of meaning called morphemes, some of which could stand alone as words and were called *free morphemes*, while others were only ever used when attached to another words (*bound morphemes*). They then looked at some words together and separated them into morphemes and Ahmed asked the learners to decide which were free morphemes and which were bound morphemes.

Ahmed told the class that many common exception words can have affixes added to change their meanings. For example, *beautiful* can become *beautifully* and *friend* can become *friends*, *friendly* and *friendlier*. He explained that the more the learners understand about morphology, the greater the range of language they can learn. They worked in groups on breaking the words into morphemes and then, in a plenary session, Ahmed collected their ideas and addressed any misconceptions, before writing examples on the board as follows:

unlikely – un(bound) + like (free) + ly (bound)

disappear – dis (bound) + appear (free)

trigraph – tri (bound) + graph (free)

supermarket – super (bound) + market (free)

minibeast – mini (bound) + beast (free)

antifreeze – anti (bound) + freeze (free)

wonderfully – wonder (free) + ful (bound) + ly (bound)

Ahmed was delighted that some learners argued that *mini* could be a free morpheme as in the name of a car or a skirt, and that *super* was also a word in its own right. He explained that sometimes prefixes did become words over time and shared some examples, including *dis* (*diss*) and *maxi*.

A Spot of Theory

The term morphology *was first used in the early nineteenth century and referred to the form and structure of plants and animals. Crystal (2005) maintains that its first recorded use in relation to words came in 1869.*

It is worth mentioning that some bound morphemes become free with usage, for example, hyper *as in 'He was a bit hyper' and* 'mini' *as in the car or skirt.*

Strategy: Reassessing opinions – it's not as hard as you think

Do you still think common exception words are tricky? Hopefully, you are already reconsidering your thoughts and approaches when it comes to common exception words. Here are a few suggested teaching techniques that will demonstrate even further that it's not as hard as you perhaps thought.

5. Creating mnemonics

Mnemonics can be a useful device for teaching common exception words. Examples include **Big Elephants Can Always Understand Small Elephants** to remember *because* and **Harry Always Laughs First** to help with *half*. Adults often use mnemonics too, including *stationery has envelopes, but a car is stationary* to recall that there is either an 'e' or an 'a' before the 'r', and that **Down In Africa Red Riding Hood Only Eats Apples** is to remind them how to spell diarrhoea! Learners enjoy making up their own mnemonics. These could be added to a working wall in the classroom for all to share.

✸ How many mnemonics do you know?

✸ Could you write one for the word *beautiful*?

6. Spelling tests with a twist

Are spelling tests still a good idea? Possibly not if delivered in the traditional format! However, there are many alternative, more successful ways to use a 'test' as a learning strategy, rather than just an isolated, meaningless activity, after which the words that are practised are often not retained.

A Spot of Theory

Jackson (1995) explained that new words enter our vocabulary in different ways. We 'borrow' them from other languages, so we get karate *and* tycoon *from Japanese;* boutique *and* discotheque *from French;* anorak *from Eskimo; and* pyjamas *from Hindi.*

Some words are derived from names, so we often talk about hoovering *when we use a vacuum cleaner, because Hoover is a major manufacturer, or we say we use a* biro *even when we use a different kind of ballpoint pen, because Biro make such pens.*

A primary school in County Durham wanted to change the way learners learned how to spell, including spelling common exception words with unusual GPCs. They still wanted to include a spelling test as one of their teaching strategies; however, they wanted it to be a much more successful and embedded element of the learning process.

On occasions where learners were given lists of words to learn for tests, the learners were given the 'test' before they saw the list they had to learn. This enabled the learners to have a go at the spellings and to identify which ones they already knew and what the tricky bits were in those they couldn't yet spell accurately. They could then focus their learning on what they actually needed to remember. By using 'tests' in this way the school removed the negative overtones and showed that they viewed them as part of a learning strategy rather than an unpleasant event for some learners at the end of the week.

Rather than teachers testing the whole class, learners worked in pairs or groups to test each other and to help each other to learn the spellings. If a test was administered, the teachers collected each group's aggregate scores rather than each individual's. This provided a real incentive for groups to work co-operatively to help everyone to succeed.

7. Let's celebrate!

It is a good idea to make common exception words part of everyday life in the classroom. They should be embraced, celebrated and mastered! They should be taught, practised, discussed, displayed, used, read, written and enjoyed.

They could be introduced on an easily accessible working wall, where both adults who worked in the class and pupils could display the unusual GPCs and common exception words that they were currently working on, or had been recently learning. This would provide a focal point where word groups, learning aids and other resources could be used for reference. Learners would soon became engaged in collecting words from all around them; from home, those they passed in the street and words they spotted around the school.

Teaching aids such as word mats and flashcards could always be easily accessible around the classroom, at work-tables and in the reading and writing areas. Games, such as snap and lotto, which were tailored to suit the common exception words that were being studied at the time, could be made available. The use of a treasure box is effective – this is a place where the common exception words could be placed and cherished when the learners have mastered them.

Strategy: Teaching techniques – it's really not that tricky

So what else can you do to successfully teach learners how to read and spell common exception words? Here are some further useful strategies and ideas, for use in the classroom.

8. Using the most common 100 words

Many of the most frequently used words in the English language have unusual GPCs in them. They are part of the spoken and written language of primary classrooms, and appear in the reading materials that learners use frequently. The amount of unusual GPCs are evident in the list of 100 most common words used in English, as seen in the table opposite.

You probably decided that words like *about*, *and*, *up*, *got*, *had*, *down* and *dad* could be sounded out; but what about *said*, *do*, *their*, *one* and *people*? These words include 'tricky' parts for readers who don't know of other words with the same letter sound correspondences. The 'ai' in *said* and the 'eo' in *people* rarely make the vowel sounds found in those words, while 'eir' in *their* can be found in a few words such as *heir*, but most of these may be unfamiliar to learners. These words can cause frustration for readers, especially as the words feature so frequently in texts.

the	are	do	about	and
up	me	got	a	had
down	their	to	my	dad
people	said	her	big	your
in	what	when	put	he
there	it's	could	I	out
see	house	of	this	looked
old	it	have	very	too
was	went	look	by	you
be	don't	day	they	like
come	made	on	some	will
time	she	so	into	I'm
is	not	back	if	for
then	from	help	at	were
children	Mrs	his	go	him
called	but	little	Mr	here
that	as	get	off	with
no	just	asked	all	mum
now	saw	we	one	came
make	can	them	oh	an

(Masterson et al, 2003)

But if you consider the list of the most common 100 words again, and group the words into those that are decodable using phonic strategies and those that have a tricky bit, you can see that only approximately 40 per cent of the words are considered to be common exception words.

A Spot of Theory

There are some words in the list of the most common 100 words that are difficult to group with others and the phonic strategies already discussed simply are not suitable. It is, therefore, sometimes the most successful strategy to teach a tricky word as the 'whole thing' so that learners can instantly recognise the word on sight. Nevertheless, we should not rely too heavily on learning whole words as a strategy in early reading.

Strategy in action

A group of Key Stage 1 teachers decided to analyse the most common 100 words to decide:

- Which words contain an unusual GPC?
- Which words contain more than one unusual GPC?
- Which words were most frequently misspelled by their classes?
- How they might teach learners to read and spell these words?

They then compared their findings with those presented in *Letters and Sounds* (DfES, 2007), as seen in the tables on the next page:

Decodable words (DfES, 2007)

a	dad	but	look	time
an	had	put	too	house
as	back	will	went	about
at	and	that	it's	your
if	get	this	from	day
in	big	then	children	made
is	him	them	just	came
it	his	with	help	make
of	not	see	don't	here
off	got	for	old	saw
on	up	now	I'm	very
can	mum	down	by	

Tricky words (DfES, 2007)

the	me	said	little	Mrs
to	be	have	one	looked
I	was	like	when	called
no	you	so	out	asked
go	they	do	what	could
into	all	some	oh	
he	are	come	their	
she	my	were	people	
we	her	there	Mr	

The teachers then considered how they might group words together to learn more than one at a time. Their grouping ideas included:

he, she, we, me, be – with an 'e' that makes the /ee/ phoneme

no, go, so – with 'o' that says its letter name

do, to – with 'o' that makes the /oo/ phoneme

can, dad, had, get, big, him, his, not, got, mum, but, put, was – CVC words

Mr, Mrs – titles that required capitalisation

time, made, came, make, here – containing split digraphs

some, come – rhyme

the, their, there, them, that, they, this, then – initial /th/ phoneme

looked, called, asked – '–ed' ending

it's, don't, I'm – containing apostrophes

an, as, at, if, in, is, it, of, on, up – a vowel followed by a consonant

to, no, go, he, we, me, be, so, do (by, my) – consonant followed by a vowel, including the alternative 'y'

✸ Can you think of three of your own groups of words from the tables opposite?

Strategy: More teaching techniques

What else might you do to teach common exception words?

9. Grouping words in other ways

Grouping words together, in order to teach more than one at a time, can be an effective strategy. Learners can begin to understand that some words have similar morphology (structure) and etymology (origins), and they can begin to build an understanding of how words work. Groups of words might be based on those that have the same unusual GPCs. For example, *here*, *there* and *where* have the same grapheme /ere/, but represent different phonemes in *here* and *there*.

The main purpose of many of the 100 most common words is to join other words in sentences, so they are called *function words*. Without them, we couldn't create sentences. Collections of functional words, those that help to structure sentences such as *because* and *many*, can be compiled and taught in relation to each other.

Content words are those which name and describe things and actions. Learners' first words tend to be content words like *mummy*, *daddy*, *drink* and *toy*, and when they first begin to recognise words around them it is usually the content words which they can first read in shops and signs. Content words, those such as *wild* and *beautiful* which add meaning and detail to sentences, can also be gathered together and taught as a group.

Words can be grouped into *homophones* and *heteronyms*. There are many examples of these in the English language.

10. Exploring homophones

There are many English words that sound the same but are spelled differently. These are called *homophones* – meaning 'same sound', from the Greek *homos* 'same', and *phone* meaning 'sound'). Look at the words below:

know	*way*	*stairs*
bored	*grown*	*waist*
waits	*write*	*mail*

Without being given a context, we wouldn't be certain to be able to spell any of the words correctly. If you heard those words without seeing them and were asked to spell them, you might write

no	*weigh*	*stares*
board	*groan*	*waste*
weights	*right*	*male*

It is important to teach learners about the context for words to help them make correct choices and therefore have a better chance at spelling the words correctly.

11. Investigating heteronyms

Heteronyms are words that are spelled the same but pronounced differently and have different meanings (from Greek *hetero* 'different' and *nym* 'name'). Consider how you would pronounce *close* and how different pronunciations would give different meanings to the word. If you say it with the 's' sounded as in *yes*, you would mean 'near', but if you sound the 's' as in *has* and *was*, you would mean 'shut'.

I didn't know where to find what to wear

I worked all week and was too weak to carry on

Molly wanted to look at homophones in a creative way and searched online to find homophone poems. She was surprised at how many were available and although some were rather weak, she found some excellent examples to share with her Year 5 class. She shared these with them and then asked the learners to help her to write a class homophone poem.

First, she displayed a long list of pairs of homophones and then asked them to work in pairs on mini whiteboards to write sentences that included pairs of homophones. Examples produced by the learners included:

> I worked all week and was too weak to carry on.
>
> I didn't know where to find something nice to wear.
>
> The building site I saw was a sight for sore eyes.

Molly wrote these and others on the interactive whiteboard and asked learners to help her to manipulate and modify them to create a coherent poem. She drew attention to the different spellings and asked for suggestions as to how these could be remembered. The class then worked in pairs to write their own homophone poems.

A Spot of Theory

Williams (2006) argues that learning whole words is not enough to become a skilled reader, as it relies on visual memory and 'the number of new words encountered soon outstrips the ability to remember them on sight' (2006, p 55). Furthermore, Stuart (2006) found that in order to enter sight vocabulary, words need to be encountered significantly more often than most words appear in everyday reading.

Use this to keep a record of what worked well for you and what didn't. A strategy that works with one learner or group of learners may not work so well with another. Keeping a checklist helps you to work out what factors or learner characteristics call for one approach rather than another. There's a line at the bottom for you to add your own most frequently used strategy, if it's not already included in the list.

Strategy	Tried it with...	On... (date)	It worked	It didn't work	Worth trying again?
1. Is the whole word tricky?					
2. Will these words always be tricky?					
3. Etymology matters					
4. Discussing morphology					
5. Creating mnemonics*					
6. Spelling tests with a twist					
7. Let's celebrate					
8. Using the most common 100 words					
9. Grouping words in other ways					
10. Exploring homophones					
11. Investigating heteronyms					
Your own strategy?					

DAY 5: Systematic teaching: planning effective lessons and assessing

What do we mean by the *systematic teaching* of phonics? In essence, phonics teaching should be explicit and discrete; it should focus only on phonics and be taught separately in lessons that are clearly demarcated from other areas of the curriculum, including English. It should be well-organised and taught in a clearly defined sequence; each lesson should closely follow the last and should build on previous knowledge and skills mastered. It should include all the sound and letter relationships or, as discussed on Day 1, all the grapheme-phoneme correspondences (GPCs).

Day 5 looks at effective ways of making phonics teaching systematic, and explores the characteristics of successful phonics lessons and planning. It discusses ways of assessing phonics, and how that assessment should inform future planning. It considers those learners who do not make expected progress in phonics, and those that may still need explicit phonics teaching in Key Stage 2. It briefly explores some of the different programmes that are available to deliver and support the teaching of phonics.

Today's strategies

* Planning for progression:
  1. Plan ahead – how to organise planning
  2. Planning units of work
  3. Inclusive teaching

* More designs on planning:
  4. One day at a time – daily lesson plans

* Features of successful teaching:
  5. Organising a successful lesson
  6. Get it together – grouping
  7. Listen up – fostering engagement

* How do I make my classroom inclusive?:
  8. The teaching kit – tools and resources
  9. Designing the classroom environment

* Assessing phonics:
  10. Daily, formative assessment
  11. Individual assessment and intervention

* Exploring phonics programmes:
  12. Letters and Sounds

* Exploring more phonics programmes:
  13. *Read, Write, Inc.*
  14. *Jolly Phonics*
  15. Other popular programmes

* Involving other adults:
  16. Involving and educating parents and colleagues
  17. Looking at the link between home and school

Strategy: Planning for progression

1. Plan ahead – how to organise planning

The Department for Education (DfE) set out criteria to ensure high-quality systematic phonics. It stipulated that:

High-quality systematic, synthetic phonic work will make sure that learners learn:

- grapheme–phoneme correspondences (the alphabetic principle) in a clearly defined, incremental sequence;
- to apply the highly important skill of blending (synthesising) phonemes, in order, all through a word to read it;
- to apply the skills of segmenting words into their constituent phonemes to spell; and that
- blending and segmenting are reversible processes.

(DfE, 2011b, pp 2–3)

To ensure phonics is systematic and is taught in a clearly defined sequence, planning should be considered in multi-level formats; perhaps termly or half-termly in units, alongside weekly and daily plans. In order to closely match the needs of the learners being taught, the outcomes from previous teaching will inform what will be taught next. These outcomes will be identified by continually assessing the learners. Assessment will be explored more closely later in this chapter.

2. Planning units of work

When considering the planning of units and weekly blocks, the overarching aims for the teaching of phonics during a set time are identified. These may of course be reconsidered and adjusted as a result of the progress made by the learners. Perhaps more time may need to be dedicated to a skill or concept that a learner has found particularly challenging, and this will need to be revisited in the next unit of work. It is expected that most learners will learn phonics at a rapid rate, and that they will have learned all GPCs and effective blending and segmenting skills by the time they complete Year 1. It is assumed that learners will at that point be ready to complete the *Phonics Screening Check*, a national phonics assessment tool. Information about the *Phonics Screening Check* can be found in Day 2. The recommended pace of instruction ensures that GPCs are introduced at the rate of between three and five a week, starting with single letters and a sound for each, then going on to the sounds represented by digraphs, eg /ch/ and /ee/ and larger grapheme units, eg /ear/, /igh/, as discussed on Day 3.

The teaching of blending of phonemes for reading, as discussed on Day 2, is included in phonics lessons, starting after the first few GPCs are taught and continued as more GPCs are introduced. To complement this, the segmenting of phonemes for spelling, also discussed on Day 2, is taught, again starting after the first few GPCs are taught and working with more GPCs as more are introduced. Learners should be taught to both read and write the GPCs being taught, and words with those GPCs in them.

The most common spellings for phonemes are taught first and then alternative sounds for spellings and alternative spellings for sounds are gradually introduced.

Strategies for reading and spelling high-frequency words that are often encountered and common exception words, as discussed on Day 4, containing unusual GPCs should be taught alongside phonically regular words.

3. Inclusive teaching

It is no secret that children learn most effectively when they play an active part in their learning. It is important to make phonics teaching interactive, engaging and stimulating. As already discussed, popular phonics programmes provide a rich variety of fast-paced activities that stimulate and engage learners. You should vary your teaching and learning approaches to suit the different learning styles of individuals, including visual, aural and kinaesthetic learners. This means providing plenty of opportunities for learning but also for language play, including games and activities which are multi-sensory, and for seeing and sharing a range of exciting and engaging texts.

A Spot of Theory

Ofsted (2010) produced a report, Reading by Six, *in which one of the key criteria identified for effective, systematic, synthetic phonics programmes is that they should:*

...use a multi-sensory approach so that children learn variously from simultaneous visual, auditory and kinaesthetic activities which are designed to secure essential phonic knowledge and skills.

(Ofsted, 2010, p 42)

Strategy: More designs on planning

4. One day at a time – daily lesson plans

Daily lesson plans should be manageable and efficient documents. They should be easily accessible and simple to understand; they should assist in the smooth running of a lesson and they may need to be used by other adults, for example TAs and HTLAs who are trained to deliver phonics teaching (this is discussed further later in this chapter). Each plan should address the needs of individual learners, outline intentions for the teaching, tasks and activities, and indicate potential opportunities for assessment.

When planning for individual daily lessons, the following opportunities should be included:

- to *revisit* previous knowledge and skills, practising again, for example, those GPCs, blending skills or common exception words that have recently been taught;

- to *teach* something new, for example, an alternative grapheme for a known phoneme, segmenting skills to read an unknown word or a tricky bit in a previously unseen common exception word;

- to *practise* the new concept or skill introduced in the lesson;

- to *apply* the new concept or skill in a useful way, for example, using a newly taught grapheme in a word, using blending skills to read an unfamiliar sentence or identifying the tricky bit in a common exception word and devising a mnemonic to help to remember it (refer back to Day 4 for a reminder about mnemonics).

Including these four elements in every phonics lesson encourages a fast-paced, well-organised session during which learners are given the opportunity to practise skills and knowledge already gained, and to learn new information. It is recommended in different programmes, some of which are explored in the next section, that each element of the lesson should last approximately five to seven minutes, and it is important that lessons are short, lively and interactive.

Strategy in action

Daniel, a newly qualified teacher in Year 1, wanted to ensure his phonics lessons always had the four key teaching elements (revisit, teach, practise, apply). The planning format given to Daniel by his school did not have the elements indicated on it, and so Daniel designed a grid, containing the four elements, that he completed alongside his planning. The grid was designed only to hold brief information so was quick to complete and easy to access. Daniel used the grid to track his teaching and the learners' progress through each element.

Revisit

Teach

Practise

Apply

Devise a phonics lesson planning grid

Strategy: Features of successful teaching

5. Organising a successful lesson

Lessons should be fairly short in length and a reasonable pace should be maintained throughout. Approximately 20 minutes is an ideal time to spend on direct phonics teaching; this gives enough time to complete several quick activities while the learners remain focused and engaged. It is expected that lessons should take place on a daily basis, and perhaps even at the same time each day, thus developing a phonics routine that both pupils and teachers are comfortable with.

6. Get it together – grouping

Learners should be grouped by ability to ensure that teaching closely matches the needs of each learner. Groups should be manageable in size, to allow each learner to receive maximum attention from the teacher, and to allow the teacher to monitor engagement and progress successfully. The size of the group will depend on the needs of the learners; however, it is expected that a group of between 6 and 12 pupils, and a maximum of 20 per group would be reasonable.

Arrangements for ability grouping may have an impact upon the organisation of the phonics teaching in a typical classroom as there may be several groups of learners who need direct phonics teaching each day. Schools who manage this well often provide training for the TAs and HTLAs who support teaching in the classroom. This means the learners can be taught and supported by a range of adults who are proficient in the teaching of phonics. Phonics lessons are sometimes timetabled in schools so that the whole of Key Stage 1 (and perhaps Key Stage 2 if needed) is taught phonics at the same time each day. This allows greater scope for

organising groups, as learners from different classes might be brought together for phonics teaching, according to their ability. Of course, this has implications for assessing and reporting, as a learner may not be being taught phonics by their usual classteacher who is responsible for the assessment procedures for that learner, and this will be addressed later in the chapter.

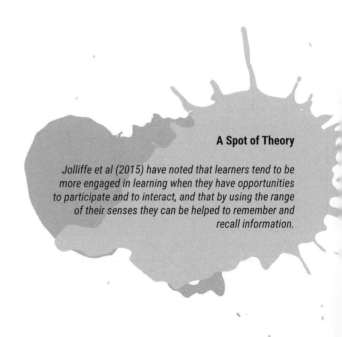

A Spot of Theory

Jolliffe et al (2015) have noted that learners tend to be more engaged in learning when they have opportunities to participate and to interact, and that by using the range of their senses they can be helped to remember and recall information.

West Lane Primary School arranged their phonics teaching so that learners from different classes were taught together, according to ability. The teachers wanted a quick method of reporting back on a learner's progress or issues to their classteacher, or other interested adults. They devised a certificate scheme, with different messages, that they would complete for a learner when needed. These were the three certificates:

* *Something I have done well* allowed a learner to celebrate a particular achievement

* *I need to think about this again* indicated that the learner needed to revisit a particular aspect, but not necessarily with the help of an adult

* *I'd like some help with this* meant that an adult should take action to give that learner further support, perhaps during a reading session or at home.

* What would you include in your phonics certificates?

7. Listen up – fostering engagement

Throughout phonics lessons, learners should be engaged in fast-paced activities that often require rapid responses. Responses may be verbal, and learners might be expected to answer or reply to the teacher's questions at the same time as the other learners, in a group response situation. Learners might be required to respond to a partner; verbalising what they have just heard can be a successful technique for remembering a new phoneme or the tricky bit of a common exception word.

Sometimes responses might require short written answers, perhaps when learners are asked to practise writing a grapheme, write that grapheme in a word or when they are making an attempt to spell a common exception word. Learners are often expected to write small letters in a restricted space in more formal workbooks and on worksheets; however, they often benefit from experimenting with writing letters and graphemes in other situations and with the freedom of producing many sizes of letters. Whiteboards and wipeable pens are ideal tools for this; responses are 'temporary' and can be easily edited, which allows learners to try out and refine techniques quickly and without the need for the best quality presentation. It should however be noted that research shows that there is a clear link between spelling and handwriting, particularly cursive 'joined' handwriting; that spelling can become automatic and 'flow' from the pen as joins are made between letters in digraphs and other grapheme units. It has been found that, often, when we write common graphemes and letter strings, for instance 'th', 'ch' and 'ing', we are able to write them without making a conscious effort to do so. It is therefore important that learners are taught to ensure that writing outcomes in phonics are presented with high standards of penmanship. We will look at using a variety of media and medium for writing in the next section.

Strategy: How do I make my classroom inclusive?

8. The teaching kit – tools and resources

It is important to consider what learners both write with, and write on, while engaged in phonic activities.

Media to write with might include a variety of pens, pencils and crayons, with different thicknesses and colours. Paint, chalk, glue and other artist materials can produce letters and words with different textures that learners might then trace. Magnetic letters and shapes are useful for quick word-play activities. Keyboards, interactive whiteboards, tablets and other electronic devices are useful and accessible ways for learners to access and record phonics. The ability to be able to alter text size, shape and colour is a particular benefit of using a multi-modal approach.

When considering media to write on, it is important to offer a wide variety of paper to write on, varying in colour, thickness, size and texture. This gives the learners a variety of visual effects as they form chosen letters, graphemes and words. Allow learners to trace letters, graphemes and words in the air, both following letter shapes that they can see, and independently without a shape to trace. Learners can be encouraged to use their 'writing finger', which is usually part of their preferred writing hand (the hand they hold their pencil with). Tools and fingers can be used to scratch letters into modelling materials. If clay is used, this can be used for printing once dry. Learners can use their bodies, individually and in groups, perhaps during PE or in a larger space than the classroom, to make letter shapes.

9. Designing the classroom environment

Another key thing to consider is the learning environment. Classroom displays, labels and signs can all contribute to supporting the teaching of phonics and early reading. Clear, large lettering in a suitable and consistent font will make written text around the classroom more accessible to learners, while well-placed letter and phoneme posters or signs will give learners a continual point of reference to check their own understanding. Sand trays, carpeting and other textured surfaces can be made available so that learners can trace and feel the letter shapes.

Learners can contribute to phonics-based displays by producing large colourful letters, graphemes and words using a range of writing and drawing media. Sticky notes with graphemes, common exception words and other related items can be added to an interactive display, ideally placed lower in the classroom at a child-friendly height. A dedicated display for phonics-based programmes is a useful area in the classroom to continually enhance phonics teaching and to allow learners access to visual clues and key information to support their learning. In addition to the main teaching areas in the classroom, many teachers provide spaces for learners to practise and experiment with phonics and spelling, for example, role-play areas with frequently changed themes, and construction, modelling, painting and writing areas.

The classrooms at The Hill Infants School did not have dedicated phonics areas. The phonics subject leader of the school visited other schools in the local area that had developed good practice in this. She then developed an area in her own classroom, with many of the successful elements she had seen in other schools, including a 'sticky note' station for adding new graphemes and tricky words, different media for practising phonics, a focus spot for phoneme/grapheme of the week and books for practising decoding skills. She then invited the other teachers in her school to develop dedicated phonics areas in their own classrooms.

Draw a design of the interactive dedicated phonics area for your classroom.

Is your phonics area in need of some tender care and attention?

Strategy: Assessing phonics

10. Daily, formative assessment

As mentioned earlier in the chapter, when discussing how planning should be organised, information collected from the daily assessment of individual learners should inform the planning of the next lesson. Phonics teaching should be sequential, closely matched to learners' ability and should build on previously learned skills and knowledge. It is important that each stage has been achieved to ensure that the learners are confident and fluent and ready to progress to the next stage. It is also important to ensure that frequent opportunities to review phonemes are taught – it is this process of 'over-learning' that is so important for successful phonics acquisition. Teachers should also take the opportunity to consistently evaluate their phonics teaching, to ensure lessons are challenging, engaging and appropriate.

If a learner has not mastered an element of phonics, they should revise and apply it again until effective progress has been made. It is crucial that learners have meaningful opportunities to practise, consolidate and extend their phonic skills and knowledge in a broad range of contexts. Judgements should be made, through observations during phonics lessons about learners' progress and achievement, so that informed decisions can be made about future planning.

Records should be kept of the progress of individuals. These should be easy to update and access. This is key to tracking pupils' achievements and learning needs, setting future targets and areas for development and reporting to colleagues, parents and other interested adults.

11. Individual assessment and intervention

Where teachers have not been able to gather sufficient information from observations to provide a clear picture of learners' achievements, or have concerns about a particular learner, a more focused adult-led assessment must be undertaken. Decisions can then be taken about intervention activities, designed to support those not making expected progress in particular aspects of phonics. Those who are making better-than-expected progress can also be identified and appropriate provision can be made. Intervention should not necessarily mean teaching those learners as identified with additional needs separately from those accessing core phonics teaching. It is important to consider carefully before withdrawing learners from whole-class phonics teaching if they seem to be achieving below the expected rate of progression. These learners may benefit from the whole-class experience of blending and segmenting and hearing a range of phonemes, in addition to vocabulary development. Further support may be provided individually or in small groups as necessary to supplement this. Some of the phonics programmes explored in the next strategy, including *Letters and Sounds* and *Read, Write, Inc.* have specific intervention materials to support core teaching.

Although it is expected that learners will have completed specific phonics lessons in Key Stage 1, and are able to use phonic strategies independently, those learners that have not made expected progress might need phonics teaching in Key Stage 2. It is essential that learners are not simply given more of the same teaching and learning they received in Key Stage 1. Even though their reading skills may not have reached the level expected for their age group, their maturity levels will have advanced and they may find the kinds of texts that were used in Key Stage 1 are not engaging and motivating. It is important that you provide phonics teaching and reading materials that will both interest learners and help them to develop their phonemic awareness.

However, phonics teaching at Key Stage 2 is not simply for those learners who have not made expected progress. It is also an opportunity to explore further GPCs and to learn more about our language. The teaching and learning of phonics at Key Stage 2 focuses on spelling, and on supporting not only learners' reading, but also their writing. As Rose (2006) maintains, at Key Stage 2 the focus shifts from learning to read to reading to learn.

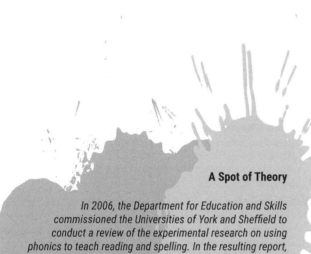

A Spot of Theory

In 2006, the Department for Education and Skills commissioned the Universities of York and Sheffield to conduct a review of the experimental research on using phonics to teach reading and spelling. In the resulting report, Torgerson et al found that systematic phonics teaching:

...enables children to make better progress in reading accuracy than unsystematic or no phonics, and that this is true for both normally-developing children and those at risk of failure.

(Torgerson et al, 2006, p 45)

Strategy: Exploring phonics programmes

The Rose Review (2006) noted that a phonics programme should be followed with *'fidelity'*. As Jolliffe et al (2015) have noted, the issue of the fidelity to a programme has created some confusion, and a commonly held interpretation is that teaching should be restricted to one phonics programme, as long as that programme meets the criteria for high-quality phonics work. However, the term refers more broadly to fidelity to a framework or structure. The key, therefore, is that although an entire framework should be covered, it does not mean that this needs to be restricted to one specific programme. Some of the popular phonics programmes that are used in primary classrooms are briefly discussed below. In practice, schools often find that adhering to one programme that meets the criteria for high-quality phonics teaching ensures that this happens. The important issue, no matter how phonics teaching is delivered, is that teaching should be carefully structured and it should enable learners' progress to be clearly assessed and monitored.

12. Letters and Sounds

Letters and Sounds is a phonics programme, published by the DfES (2007), and is commonly used in primary schools. It is free to use and is easily obtainable; the documents are available online and many websites have been developed to support the programme, offering resources, display materials, games and activities, planning and assessment ideas and much more. *Letters and Sounds* divides the teaching of phonics into six phases, with suggested teaching strategies and resources provided for each phase:

* Phase One *is designed to be used with early readers in EYFS. It supports linking sounds and letters in the order in which they occur in words, and naming and sounding the letters of the alphabet.*

* Phase Two *is designed to last up to six weeks, and should be completed by most learners in EYFS. The purpose of this phase is to teach at least 19 letters, and move learners on from oral blending and segmentation to blending and segmenting with letters.*

* Phase Three *has a suggested time frame of up to 12 weeks, and should be completed by most learners in EYFS. The purpose of this phase is to teach another 25 graphemes, most of them comprising digraphs, so the learners can represent each of about 42 phonemes by a grapheme.*

* Phase Four *should take four to six weeks to complete, and might be completed by most learners in EYFS. The purpose of this phase is to consolidate learners' knowledge of graphemes in reading and spelling words containing adjacent consonants and polysyllabic words.*

* Phase Five *is designed to be taught throughout Year 1. The purpose of this phase is for learners to broaden their knowledge of graphemes and phonemes for use in reading and spelling.*

* Phase Six *is designed to be taught throughout Year 2 and focuses on applying the phonics knowledge and skills developed in previous phases. During this phase, learners should become fluent readers and increasingly accurate spellers.*

(DfES, 2007)

Amy, a third-year trainee, was preparing to work with a Year 2 class for her final placement, but knew little about *Letters and Sounds*. She discussed her situation with her tutor, who showed her teaching materials and six phases. He then arranged to take Amy into a school where the teachers were well established in using it. She observed lessons and talked with the teachers and phonics subject leader about the programme and the way in which it was taught. It was agreed that she would observe lessons with different groups and would gradually take on some of the teaching of parts of lessons. The school was impressed by Amy's knowledge of the terminology associated with phonics in general and with *Letters and Sounds*.

A Spot of Theory

The Rose Review (2006), which informed the government in their decision to introduce phonics teaching in primary schools, focused on ensuring the systematic teaching of phonics, emphasising the importance of teaching a systematic structured progression. It stated that:

...phonic work should teach these skills and knowledge in a well-defined and systematic sequence.

(para 45–6)

The report also stated that such teaching should be:

...systematic, that is to say, it follows a carefully planned programme with fidelity, reinforcing and building on previous learning to secure children's progress.

(para 45–6)

Strategy: More phonics programmes

13. *Read, Write, Inc.*

Read, Write, Inc. is a popular commercial scheme used widely in primary schools. The programme developers recommend training, for teachers and other adults involved in using the scheme. There are five key principles that schools are expected to follow: pace, praise, purpose, participation and passion.

The programme teaches all the GPCs, or *speed sounds*, using picture clues and mnemonics. Phonically decodable words, those with common GPCs, are known as *green words*, and common exception words are known as *red words*. The programme is accompanied by sets of graded books, both fiction and non-fiction, that match the level that a learner is working at. These allow learners to practice the green words and red words they are learning, and to develop the blending and segmenting skills needed to read.

There are many resources and display materials available, including grapheme friezes, speed sound charts and software for the interactive whiteboard. Handbooks and lesson plans are provided. There are a variety of programmes available that complement *Read, Write, Inc.*: *Get Writing!* is designed to teach writing and spelling to learners who are already working on the core phonics programme; there are intervention materials for those learners not making expected progress on the core *Read, Write, Inc.* programme; and *Fresh Start* is a phonics programme designed to teach learners in Key Stage 2.

14. *Jolly Phonics*

Jolly Phonics focuses on 42 GPCs (compared with 44 for *Letters and Sounds* and *Read, Write, Inc.*). The GPCs are split into seven groups, which are learned in a specific order. As with other programmes, this is designed to enable learners to begin building words as early as possible. A distinctive feature of *Jolly Phonics* is the use of actions designed to help learners remember the letters. For example, actions include weaving the hand in an 's' shape, like a snake, and saying 'sssss'.

Jolly Phonics identifies five key skills for reading and writing:

> *Learning the letter sounds: Learners are taught 42 main letter sounds.*
>
> *Learning letter formation: Learners use multi-sensory methods to learn how to form and write the letters.*
>
> *Blending: They blend the sounds together to read and write new words.*
>
> *Identifying the sounds in words: They identify sounds in words to help with spelling.*
>
> *Tricky words (common exception words): Tricky words with irregular spellings and GPCs are learned separately.*

15. Other popular programmes

There are many other commercially available programmes available, including *Phonics Bug*, *Letterland* and *Sounds-Write*. These schemes can provide guidelines for planning and assessment, ideas for tasks and activities, resources and teaching aids. Online resources and software for interactive whiteboards accompany many of the programmes.

The phonics subject leader of a large infant school wanted to refine the way phonics was taught in his school. The school felt that using only one phonics programme, as they had been for a number of years, limited the breadth of their phonics teaching. They wanted to explore other options and so the phonics subject leader visited schools that were successfully using a range of different programmes, and had effectively adapted them to suit the needs of their learners. The subject leader was able to use the good practice he had seen to inform the choices the school made in designing a bespoke phonics curriculum that closely matched the needs of their pupils.

Strategy: Involving other adults

16. Involving and educating parents and colleagues

It is important that all adults who teach learners phonics are following the same structured sequence, have an understanding of the subject and are using the same terminology and teaching strategies. This may mean that for TAs, HTLAs and parents, training, support and guidance may need to be provided. Many adults were not taught to read using phonics and so it may not be a natural approach for them.

In order to inform and involve all adults about phonics and how to approach it, leaflets and other guidance materials might be provided, alongside recommendations for high-quality online materials where activities and games can be accessed, as well as websites that provide explanations and demonstrations of successful strategies and the correct pronunciations of phonemes. Phonics information meetings and 'open' phonics lessons, where adults are invited and can observe and be involved in activities and games, can be used to model good practice.

17. Looking at the link between home and school

A considerable amount of research has been carried out in the last four decades on the impact of the links between home and school. This has ranged from work that identifies the rich and varied literacy experiences of young learners at home and, conversely, the gulf between home and school practices. The vital importance of the support from home has been identified and the importance of working with parents in developing learners' literacy and phonics skills is crucial as this helps make meaningful links between home and school. There are many simple things that parents can do at home with their children, even before formal phonics teaching begins. For example, language is developed through everyday conversation; books and other multi-modal reading formats (such as e-readers and other devices) can be shared; marks can be made on different media; and letters and names and other simple words can be written together.

A rural primary school in the North East knew that a large proportion of the parents and carers of the learners in the school were unsure about phonics and how to support their children. They also understood that the local accent and dialect had an impact on how words and phonemes might be pronounced. The school developed a scheme for parents and carers, to inform them about phonics and how to successfully help their children. They developed leaflets explaining terminology and strategies, and giving examples of the different phonics elements. They held information meetings and invited parents and carers into school to take part in phonics lessons. They directed parents to online tools that demonstrated the enunciation of phonemes, while still embracing the peculiarities of the local pronunciation.

Parents and carers can also be encouraged to support their learner who is a confident and independent reader. A child who can read confidently can still learn a great deal from interaction with adults through reading. Discussions about what a child has read can further develop their understanding. Parents and carers might then suggest other books that may interest the learner, perhaps recommending ones they have read themselves. They can be excellent role models for the independent reader in their family; by seeing an adult reading regularly in the home the learner sees that it's a pleasurable and worthwhile activity that is celebrated and encouraged.

Practising the tricky bits of common exception words, using graphemes in different words and helping to choose the correct alternative grapheme are all simple ways that parents and carers can be encouraged to support learners with their segmenting skills for spelling. They may need to be introduced to the idea that the traditional spelling test my not be the most appropriate approach from learners, and this can be done through the Parent's Information Meetings previously mentioned.

Parents and carers can be encouraged to support the readers in their care in more practical ways; by taking learners to the local library and book shops, by providing simple materials to write and draw with and by providing regular time to allow reading and writing to happen in the home.

Checklist

Use this to keep a record of what worked well for you and what didn't. A strategy that works with one learner or group of learners may not work so well with another. Keeping a checklist helps you to work out what factors or learner characteristics call for one approach rather than another. There's a line at the bottom for you to add your own most frequently used strategy, if it's not already included in the list.

Strategy	Tried it with …	On … (date)	It worked	It didn't work	Worth trying again?
1. Plan ahead – how to organise planning					
2. Planning units of work					
3. Inclusive teaching					
4. One day at a time – daily lesson plans					
5. Organising a successful lesson*					
6. Get it together – grouping					
7. Listen up – fostering engagement					
8. The teaching kit – tools and resources					
9. Designing the classroom environment					
10. Daily, formative assessment					
11. Individual assessment and intervention					
12. *Letters and Sounds*					
13. *Read, Write, Inc.*					
14. *Jolly Phonics*					
15. Other popular programmes					
16. Involving and educating parents and colleagues					
17. Looking at the link between home and school					
Your own strategy?					

DAY 6: Phonics and spelling

Introduction

We have seen in earlier sections that English presents us with several challenges when we learn to read and write. Accurate spelling is a challenge in English, yet some people are good at spelling and rarely make mistakes. Today, you will see some of the strategies which you can use to develop both your own and your pupils' spelling. It is important that you actually *teach* spelling and provide learners with strategies so that they can develop their spelling, rather than simply giving them lists of words to learn and then testing them.

Phonic knowledge and phonological awareness do not provide everything we need to be able to spell well, but they continue to be important even for adults. Think of the times when you have written a name of a person or company you have been told on the phone: you either make an informed guess based upon your phonemic awareness or you have to ask for the spelling.

Good phonemic awareness enables learners to write longer words, sounding them out phoneme by phoneme and syllable by syllable in order, and to make a plausible phonic representation of the target word. Where phonemic awareness is weak, learners may make attempts at words which are nothing like the intended word, and which cannot be read by them or anyone else. A key strategy is to say a word slowly and check that each sound has a grapheme to represent it.

Today's strategies

- Phonics and spelling:
  1. Understanding the challenges in English spelling
  2. Knowing the strategies good spellers use
- Learning to spell:
  3. How can you teach spellings?
- Adjacent consonants:
  4. Understanding adjacent consonants
  5. CVCC words and how to teach them
  6. CCVC words and how to teach them
- Morphology
  7. How to teach morphology
- Prefixes
  8. Understanding and teaching prefixes
- Suffixes
  9. Understanding and teaching suffixes
- Compound words
  10. How to teach compound words
- Using phonics in later spelling development
  11. Understanding spelling rules and generalisations

Strategy: Phonics and spelling

1. Understanding the challenges in English spelling

In order to spell, we need to understand the alphabetic system – the correspondence between letters and sounds. However, in English, unlike in some other languages such as Finnish, there are lots of variations in the ways in which many phonemes can be represented. In the words below, you can see that the same vowel sound /aw/ can be represented using six different graphemes, including three digraphs (*aw*, *or*, *au*), a trigraph (*our*), and two quadgraphs (*augh*, *ough*):

> *jaw   horn   bought   taught   taunt   mourn*

When writing, we have to choose the appropriate spelling for each sound. This can still be challenging for more experienced readers, but they tend to know the possible spellings for sounds, while beginner readers and writers may have a more limited range of graphemes to choose from and so often make mistakes.

2. Knowing the strategies good spellers use

Good spellers use four main approaches when they attempt to spell a word:

- Phonic (spelling it the way it sounds) – this often produces a correct spelling, but sometimes graphemes are chosen which are phonically possible but incorrect, as in the following: 'independant' for *independent*; 'seperate' for *separate* and 'wotch' for *watch*.

- Analogy – drawing upon knowledge of other spellings. Thus, when asked to spell *fright* we might think of *night*, *right* and *sight*.

- Knowledge of root words – thus when asked to spell *definitely*, if we know that the root is *finite* we would be less likely to make the common mistake of spelling it 'definately'.

- Visual – this can be particularly helpful for those who read a lot and involves writing a word with different spellings before deciding which one looks right.

When learners begin to write, they start to use marks or letters to represent the sounds they can hear in words. As we saw in Day 1, they often make mistakes and this is understandable since their knowledge of which graphemes match which phonemes is still developing. If they are to write independently, they need to:

- Hear the separate phonemes, or sounds, in words (for example, the four phonemes in *barks*: /b/ar/k/s/) in the correct order. We call this segmenting.

- Match a letter or letters, or grapheme, to each phoneme.

Look at the piece of writing produced by a Year 1 child and notice how she has matched letters to sounds.

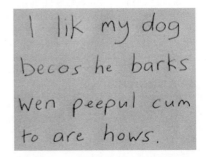

Assuming Harriet *likes* rather than *licks* her dog, 'lik' is the only word which is not phonically plausible because the long vowel sound is only represented by 'i'. When we analyse Harriet's writing we might decide to focus on split digraphs with her to enable her to improve that aspect of her spelling. We can, of course, teach her the correct spellings for *because*, *when*, *people* and *come*, as well as explaining the difference between *are* and *our*, but we might not wish to do all of this at once.

As we have seen already, in English almost every phoneme can be represented in more than one way and so it is understandable that learners (and adults) sometimes make the wrong choices. Some phonics programmes produce charts which show the main possible representations for each of the approximately 44 phonemes in English. The graphemes can be accompanied by words which include them and even pictures, for example:

> *b, bb – bag, rabbit*

> *c, k, ck, ch – cat, kit, back, school*

As learners' vocabulary develops, such charts can be added to so that the /k/ sound is also represented by /cc/ in *account*, /q/ in *queen* etc.

Asif wanted to produce a grapheme chart with his Year 1 class so that they could have a growing resource as they learned more grapheme-phoneme correspondences (GPCs). He began by displaying, in alphabetical order, the graphemes they had already learned and then asked learners to suggest words which included these letters at the beginning or end. He wrote the words on card in black, but with the focused grapheme in red. The chart grew as learners suggested new words and as new GPCs were learned. Asif found that the chart was a useful resource to use at the beginning of discrete phonics lessons, as well as incidentally during lessons when he wanted to focus on a particular spelling.

Strategy: Learning to spell

3. How can you teach spellings?

Taking lists of spellings home to learn for a test can engage learners with spelling, but only if it is part of a programme of actually *teaching* spellings and providing strategies for learning spellings. It is particularly important to look at the words learners are to learn and to talk about:

- meanings of the words and how they are used in context;
- GPCs in the words;
- pronunciation of the words;
- any 'tricky' parts of the words (see Day 4);
- strategies for remembering how to spell the words;
- words which can be derived from the words by adding morphemes (eg *usual: unusual, usually, unusually*).

Some simple strategies can be modelled by teachers, so that learners draw upon them naturally when they are learning to spell.

Look-say-cover-write-check

The most frequently used strategy links to all of the other strategies described. It simply involves looking carefully at a word, saying it aloud, covering it up, then writing it down from memory, before checking whether you spelled it correctly. If you did, then move on to another word. If not, go through the process again, focusing on the bits you got wrong until you spell the word correctly.

Blending and segmenting

As part of the *look-say-cover-write-check* process, it is important to pronounce words correctly. Teachers can help by saying words aloud and enunciating carefully, reading the word at normal speed and also reading it slowly to emphasise each phoneme. By segmenting words into their individual sounds (phonemes), we can draw attention to the letters (graphemes) which represent each sound. For example, when learning to spell *apparent* you might emphasise each phoneme as follows: /a/ pp/a/r/e/n/t/. A likely spelling error would be to put an *a* rather than an *e* for the fifth phoneme, so you could emphasise the sound here as /e/ as in *bent* or *rent*.

A Spot of Theory

Even if you learned 20 spellings a week for a 40-week school year, you would only know 800 spellings. If you spend 14 years at school and never learned any word twice, you would still only have learned 11,200 words. Crystal (2009) maintained that the average adult has a vocabulary of 35,000 to 50,000 words, so it is not possible to learn all of these words by rote: we need strategies to help us.

Identify and learn the 'tricky' bits

Most people learning to spell *apparent* will need to focus on the *e* and possibly also the double *pp*. These are the 'tricky' parts of the word (see Day 4). Such 'tricky' bits are common in English and it helps if we identify them when making our first attempts at writing the words. Look at the words below from the Year 3–4 spelling list and identify the bits which might be tricky for some spellers:

answer

calendar

build

Over-syllabification

In the examples above, you would probably emphasise the *w* in *answer*, perhaps by sounding it even though it is not voiced when we say the word. This is called over-syllabification and is a strategy we tend to use when there are unvoiced letters in words which make them tricky to spell. Think about how you remember how to spell *Wednesday* and *raspberry*: you probably say, in your head or even aloud, *Wed-nes-day* and *rasp-berry*.

Syllables

As spelling develops and learners are more confident with individual GPCs, they tend to chunk groups of sounds when reading and spelling. For longer words, this might involve separating words into syllables and then matching sounds to letters to spell. For example, *ex-per-im-ent*, *pop-u-lar*, *sep-ar-ate*.

Analogy

Words with similar spellings can be learned as groups, for example *ditch*, *pitch*, *witch*, *hitch*, *stitch* and *cloud*, *proud*, *aloud*. This enables learners to see frequent spelling patterns and helps once they have mastered individual GPCs.

Morphemes

We will look at morphology in more detail later, but it is important to be able to identify the base or root word within a word and learn the different morphemes (units of meaning) and their spellings, for example: *unhelpful = un-help-ful*; *carefully = care-ful-ly*.

Mnemonics

Mnemonics help us recall things like the colours of the rainbow (*Richard of York gave battle in vain – red, orange, yellow, green, blue, indigo, violet*). They can also be useful for remembering the tricky bits of words. For example, *separate* is very often misspelled as 'seperate', but if you remember that sep**arat**e has *a rat* in it, you'll remember to use an *e* rather than an *a* in the middle of the word. Other examples include: *accommodate has double beds* to remember that there are double letters, and *I should be embarrassed if I put two Rs in harassed*, to recall that one word has two Rs while the other has one.

Strategy: Adjacent consonants

4. Understanding adjacent consonants

On Day 3 you learned that consonant digraphs are different from adjacent consonants. Digraphs are single phonemes made by putting two letters together, for example *sh* in *shop*. In adjacent consonants we can still hear both (or sometimes all three) letter sounds, for example in *flood*, *stop*, *strap* and *scrap*.

As learners move on from learning CVC words (for example, *cat* and *kit*), they will encounter simple CVCC (for example, *cast and kilt*) and CCVC words (for example, *blast* and *crop*), and this will give them experience of consonant blends or *adjacent consonants*. In the past, consonant blends were taught early and learners learned *onsets* and *rimes*; for example taking a blend such as *bl* and finding rimes which could be added to make words: *black*, *blush*, *blow* and *blood*. Currently, blends are not usually taught until learners can master sounding each phoneme throughout a word, as this is argued to embed careful segmenting and blending and lead to more accurate reading and spelling. Later the teacher might take a word like *men* and sound it with the learners (/m/e/n/) and then add 'd' to make *mend*, again sounding all the phonemes (/m/e/n/d/).

5. CVCC words and how to teach them

CVCC words have four sounds: *consonant, vowel, consonant, consonant*. Remember that there are four separate sounds as in *lift* (/l/i/f/t/) and that in words which include a digraph (for example, *lush* (/l/u/sh/) the two consonants at the end make a single sound – such words are not CVCC, but CVC words. Examples of CVCC words for different adjacent consonant blends include:

–ft	loft lift left
–ld –lf	elf shelf wolf held old cold
–lk –lp	milk hulk gulp help
–lt	melt belt felt
–mp	limp lump jump
–nd	hand pond send
–nk	tank bank sink
–nt	sent hunt went
–sk	desk dusk rusk
–st	just nest rest
–ct –pt –xt	fact kept next

6. CCVC words and how to teach them

CCVC words have four sounds: *consonant, consonant, vowel, consonant*. Remember that there are four separate sounds as in *stop* (/s/t/o/p/) and that in words which include a digraph (for example, *shop* (/sh/o/p/) the two consonants at the beginning make a single sound. Examples of CCVC words for different adjacent consonant blends include:

bl– br–	black blob brick brim
cl– cr–	club clock crab crop
dr–	drip drop dress

fl– fr–	flap flat frog from
gl– gr–	glad glass grin gran
pl– pr–	plus plan prod press
sc– sk–	scab scan skip skin
sm– sn–	smug smock snug snap
sp–	spit spin spot
st– sw–	step stop swing swam
tr– tw–	trim trip twig twin

We saw on Day 1 how learners reduce clusters and syllables in their early speech (Bowen, 2011), and might say *poon* for *spoon* and *keen* for *clean*. Because it is important that they hear every sound in a word if they are to have a good chance of spelling it correctly, we need to focus on careful segmentation. This can be a challenge for experienced readers who sometimes regard consonant blends as single sounds because they are so familiar with certain combinations of letters. Remember that if your mouth changes shape or your tongue moves when you are sounding phonemes, you are almost certainly saying more than one phoneme. Try saying the following consonant blends aloud and pay particular attention to the movements in your mouth: *sl*, *st*, *tr*, *fr*, *bl*, *tw*, *sc*, *dr*, *gl*, *pr*, *pl*.

Activity: Segmenting words with adjacent consonants

Look at the selection of words below which include adjacent consonants, and segment them and write each in the grapheme grid. *Stamp* and *flash* have been done for you.

trip *sleep* *field* *strong* *treat* *float* *crutch* *branch*

s	t	a	m	p
f	l	a	sh	

Answers

You should have segmented the words as follows:

s	t	a	m	p
f	l	a	sh	
t	r	i	p	
s	l	ee	p	
f	ie	l	d	
s	t	r	o	ng
t	r	ea	t	
f	l	oa	t	
c	r	u	tch	
b	r	a	n	ch

Note that *ng* is usually taught as a single sound, although in some accents both the *n* and the *g* are sounded; *tch* is a trigraph because the three letters come together to make one sound; and *wr* is a single phoneme, as in *wrong*, *wrap* and *write*.

Strategy: Morphology

7. How to teach morphology

In order to read and spell accurately, it is important to develop not only a broad vocabulary, but also an understanding of how words work. Initially, this involves relating letters to sounds to decode and encode, but learners quickly learn to add to words to modify them, for example by adding *s* or *es* to make plurals, even before they are able to read or write. If you have young children, try making up names for creatures you draw for them. You don't need to write the names down, but you will probably find that if you say, for instance, 'this is a *vup* and here's another one; now we have two…', the child will say *vups*. Similarly, if you draw a creature and call it a *vutch* and ask what we would call two such creatures, the child will say *vutches*. So even before they start school, children usually know that they can modify words by adding suffixes, even though they don't know what the suffixes look like.

It is logical, then, that once learners have acquired some basic phonic knowledge and have begun to read and write they should learn how to add prefixes and suffixes to words. The English national curriculum for England (DfE, 2013) requires learners to understand the following about prefixes (and suffixes) at different stages:

Year	
1	Add prefixes and suffixes: ✸ using the spelling rule for adding −*s* or −*es* as the plural marker for nouns and the third person singular marker for verbs ✸ using the prefix *un*− ✸ using −*ing*, −*ed*, −*er* and −*est* where no change is needed in the spelling of root words (eg *helping, helped, helper, eating, quicker, quickest*)
3–4	Apply their growing knowledge of root words, prefixes and suffixes (etymology and morphology) … both to read aloud and to understand the meaning of new words they meet
5–6	Apply their growing knowledge of root words, prefixes and suffixes (morphology and etymology) … both to read aloud and to understand the meaning of new words that they meet

Support for Spelling (DCSF, 2009) identifies five key aspects of morphological knowledge.

1. Root words. They contain one morpheme and cannot be broken down into smaller grammatical units. Examples are words such as *chair*, *man* or *night*. These are sometimes referred to as the stem or base form.

2. Compound words are where two root words combine to make a word. Examples are words like *waterfall*, *tablecloth* and *flowerbed*.

3. Suffixes are added after root words, and change the spelling and meaning of a word. Examples are *walk – walking*, *skip – skipped*, *happy – happiness*.

4. Prefixes are added before a root. Examples are *happy – unhappy*; *prove – disprove*; *tie – untie*.

5. Etymology (word derivations) – words in the English language come from a range of sources; understanding the origin of words helps pupils' spelling (eg *audi* relates to hearing – *audible*, *audience*, *audition*).

Our phonics programme rocks!

Strategy: Prefixes

8. Understanding and teaching prefixes

Prefixes are morphemes (single units of meaning) which can be placed at the beginning of a word to modify its meaning. It is useful to have a clear understanding of the most common prefixes and their meanings, and to know some words which include them. The table below provides this.

Common prefixes

Prefix	Prefix meaning	Example words
de–	from, down, away, reverse, opposite	defuse, decommission
dis–	not, opposite, reverse, away	dislike, disprove
ex–	out of, away from	explosion, expel
il–	not	illegible, illegal
im–	not, without	immobile, improbable
in–	not, without	inoperable, inadvisable
mis–	bad, wrong	misunderstand, misspell
non–	not	non-fiction, nonsense
pre–	before	prenatal, prehistoric
pro–	for, forward, before	propose, pronoun
re–	again, back	revisit, revise
un–	against, not, opposite	unlike, unkind

Prefixes which are used to indicate numbers

Prefix meaning	Prefix	Example words
1	uni–	unicycle: cycle with one wheel
1	mono–	monologue: long speech by one person
2	bi–	bicycle: cycle with two wheels
3	tri–	tripod: three-legged stand
4	quad–	quadrangle: four-sided shape
5	quint–	quintuplets: five babies born at a single birth
5	penta–	pentathlon: athletic event with five activities
6	hex–	hexagon: six-sided shape
6	sex–	sextuplet: one of six babies born at a single birth
7	hept–	heptagon: seven-sided shape
7	sept–	septennial: lasting for or occurring every seven years

8	octo–	octogenarian: someone between 80 and 89 years old
9	novem–	November: formerly the ninth month of the year
10	deka– or deca–	decade: period of 10 years
hundred	cent–	century: period of 100 years
hundred	hecto–	hectogram: 100 grams
thousand	milli–	millennium: period of 1,000 years
thousand	kilo–	kilometre: 1,000 metres
million	mega–	megawatt: one million watts
billion	giga–	gigawatt: one billion watts

Strategy in action

Prefix and root word snap

Connor devised a simple game to help his Year 3 class to focus on the meanings of prefixes and to reinforce their understanding of the ways in which bound and free morphemes come together to create words. He wanted to encourage learners to make use of dictionaries to find meanings and check that words exist.

He provided dictionaries and sets of cards for each group– some with prefixes on them and some with root words. After using the activity for the first time, Connor decided to provide some more advanced dictionaries so that learners could check if some of the more advanced words they created existed.

Before playing the game, Connor asked the learners to look at their words and prefixes and those of everyone else on their table and ensure they could read and understand them. He asked them to tell him of anything they were unsure about and he discussed these items with the whole class.

Each learner was given five cards, with the rest in a pile, face down, in the middle of the table. They put their cards on the table in front of them. The first learner then put a card in the middle of the table and the person on their left had an opportunity to put another card with it to make a word (this may be a prefix or a root word or even a compound word with no prefixes).

When someone made a word, they called 'snap', said the word and took the 'trick', providing that other players agree that it is a real word. If there were any disputes, learners checked in the dictionaries.

If a learner could not find a card to create a word, the next player on the left had a try and so on. If no one could make a word, the player who put the card down first took a card from the middle of the table to see if that will make a word. If not, the next player took one and so on. When no more words could be made the tricks were counted to see who had won. All the created words were written down and a list provided so that Connor could check for misconceptions and share interesting words with the class.

After a rather noisy beginning and after having to stop the class a few times to explain the rules and to arbitrate in some disputes, the lesson went well and Connor decided to adopt a similar approach when teaching suffixes.

🟊 What else could Connor teach using this strategy?

Strategy: Suffixes

9. Understanding and teaching suffixes

Groups of letters can be added to the end of words to make new words. For example, if we take the word *walk*, we can add:

 –s to make *walks*;

 –er to make *walker*;

 –ing to make *walking*;

 –ed to make *walked*.

There are two ways in which suffixes can make a new word.

A *Inflectional suffixes* change words grammatically, for example from singular to plural (*pig* to *pigs*, *watch* to *watches*), or from present to past tense (*watch* to *watched*, *skip* to *skipped*). Examples are provided below:

Common inflectional suffixes

Suffix	Example of original word	Example with suffix added	Grammatical change made
–s	ball	balls	plural
–es	watch	watches	plural
–en/–ren	ox child	oxen children	irregular plural

–s	I want	he wants	3rd person singular
–es	I stitch	he stitches	3rd person singular
–ed	I cook	he cooked	past tense past participle
–en	I take	he has taken	past participle (irregular)
–ing	I go	he is going	continuous/ progressive
–er	full	fuller	comparative
–est	full	the fullest	superlative

B *Derivational suffixes* create new meaning (*work* to *worker*, *care* to *careful*, *careful* to *carefully*) Examples are provided below:

Common derivational suffixes

Suffix	Example of original word	Example with suffix added	Change in word class
–ation	inform	inform**ation**	verb to noun
–sion	revise	revi**sion**	verb to noun
–er	clean	clean**er**	verb to noun
–cian	magic	magi**cian**	remains a noun

−ess	prince	princ**ess**	remains a noun
−ness	thick	thick**ness**	adjective to noun
−al	remove	remov**al**	verb to noun
−ary	mission	mission**ary**	remains a noun
−ment	state	state**ment**	verb to noun
−y	filth	filth**y**	noun to adjective
−al	environment	environment**al**	noun to adjective
−able	drink	drink**able**	noun to adjective
−ly	friend	friend**ly**	noun to adjective
−y	smell	smell**y**	noun to adjective
−ful	beauty	beauti**ful**	noun to adjective
−ly	helpful	help**fully**	adjective to adverb

You can see that when some suffixes are added, the spelling of the original word is modified slightly. For example, the 'e' is dropped from *remove* and *revise* when they become *removal* and *revision*. This also usually happens when '−ing' or '−ed' are added to verbs which end with 'e' such as *make*, *take*, *save*, *drive* and *type*. This can make developing an understanding of spellings for words with suffixes more challenging than for adding prefixes where the spelling of the original word is unaltered.

A Spot of Theory

Nunes and Bryant's research (2006) made a strong case for teaching and learning morphemes. They found that learners have difficulties with spelling words that cannot be predicted from the way they sound. They showed that when learners were aware of morphemes within words, spelling problems were reduced, and their vocabulary increased.

Nunes and Bryant concluded that it was important for teachers to:

● be aware of the role that morphemes play in spelling difficulties and how they can be addressed;

● systematically teach about morphemes and their role in spelling;

● promote spelling and language development by teaching about morphemes.

Strategy: Compound words

10. How to teach compound words

When we add prefixes and suffixes we take a root word or *free morpheme* (a word which can stand alone) and add *bound morphemes* (morphemes which cannot stand alone as words, for example *un–*, *de–*, *tri–*). When we create compound words we take two free morphemes and put them together, for example *playtime*, *playground*, *headteacher*, *classroom* and *packed lunch*. As you can see, learners meet such words all the time, so it is important that they understand their meanings as well as how to spell them. Compound words may be written in three different ways:

- as one word – *bedroom, lunchbox, toothbrush*
- hyphenated – *cover-up, break-in, play-off, shoot-out*
- as two words – *bus stop, post office, pop music*

Most compound words are nouns, but some are adjectives or verbs.

- nouns: *dinner table, hairbrush, handbag*
- adjectives: *fun-loving, breath-taking, awe-inspiring*
- verbs: *double-click, overtake, sunbathe*

It is important that learners are able to identify the words which go together to create compounds, since most are quite simple to spell and read and this can make spelling and reading long words less daunting.

Strategy in action

Alice wanted to develop her Year 2 class's understanding of compound words so she made cards of common free morphemes as follows:

head	hair	brush	teacher
tooth	house	green	farm
school	snow	fall	water
day	class	break	ache
fall	ball	foot	rain
time	play	home	work
snow	man	room	class

She ensured that everyone could read all of the words by showing them one by one and asking learners to segment and then blend them. She then gave the cards out, one to each learner, and divided them into four groups of seven. Alice asked the learners to sit in circles and put their words in front of them so that everyone could see them and then decide, as a group, if any could be put together to make compound words. After a few minutes she asked if any groups had made words and then asked each learner, in turn, whose word had not been made into part of a compound, to stand up and show it to the class. Then she asked if anyone had a word which could be joined to it. Alice wrote all the discovered words on the board and talked about what each meant. Learners spotted that several words could be part of more than one compound.

Alice asked the learners to choose any five of the compound words they had discovered as a class and write five sentences which included them. These were discussed in a plenary session and Alice then asked learners to look out for examples of compound words both in school and at home with parents and carers. She challenged them to bring at least five examples to school the next day to share with the class.

It is important to involve parents and carers whenever possible and this can extend beyond helping their children with spelling and reading. By providing specific challenges such as Alice's, teachers can keep parents informed about what their children are learning and encourage them to support the teacher's work out of school.

Dancer   Dance   Dancing

Root words

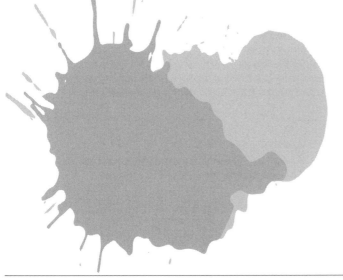

Strategy: Using phonics in later spelling development

Good phonemic awareness enables learners to write longer words, sounding them out syllable by syllable in order and to make plausible phonic representations. Where phonemic awareness is weak, learners may make attempts at words which are nothing like the intended word, and which cannot be read by anyone else. A key strategy is to say a word slowly and check that each sound has a grapheme to represent it.

11. Understanding spelling rules and generalisations

Some people are sceptical about spelling rules and cite the most well-known, *i before e except after c*, as a "rule" which has so many exceptions that it isn't worth learning (think of *their*, *science*, *reign*, *leisure*, *height*, *weight* etc). The 'rule' is probably well known because it rhymes rather than because it is very helpful, but several generalisations work well and are worth learning. Can you devise generalisations for each of the following?

A   Which letters are not used to end English words?

B   What do you do to make a noun ending with *y* plural?

C   Which letter almost always follows *q*?

D   Do any English words begin with a double consonant, for example, *bb*, *dd*, *ff*, *gg*, *hh*?

E   Which consonant digraphs do not appear at the beginning of words?

Strategy in action

Yvonne often found that learners in her Year 5 class misspelled words which they had recently got right in their weekly spelling tests. Most of the words were from the Year 5–6 spelling lists in the national curriculum. Yvonne discussed this with the class and some learners suggested that the reason they spelled some words incorrectly was because they didn't have a way of remembering the spellings in the long term. Yvonne suggested that they could try a new approach to the spellings for an experimental period of four weeks:

- Giving a 'test' on the list of words before learners were asked to copy them down to learn. This would enable them to know which parts of the words they already knew and which contained tricky parts which they would need to focus upon and remember. For example, in *leisure* some learners missed out the *i*.

- Spending more time using the words in context so that learners got used to writing them and seeing them spelled correctly.

- Having short, impromptu spelling activities where words were given out on cards and learners learned them together and then tested each other.

The strategies were effective and learners particularly liked the pre-learning tests, which were conducted in an informal way and led to lots of discussion about spelling. Yvonne and her class decided to continue this strategy and Yvonne also resolved to spend more time discussing spellings.

Answers

A   *v*, *j* and *q*

B   If a consonant precedes the *y*, remove the *y* and add *–ies* (eg *babies*); if a vowel precedes the *y* just add an *s* (eg *toys*)

C   *u*

D   No, although *llama*, a foreign word, is in the dictionary

E   *ck*, *ng*

A Spot of Theory

It is important to analyse pupils' spelling mistakes in order to identify appropriate strategies to support them. Moats identified three broad types of spelling errors pupils make and offers possible teaching strategies to support pupils:

Type of spelling error	Phonological – errors where attempts at spelling are not phonologically plausible. eg writing 'frist' for first or 'gaj' for garage. Such errors may indicate that pupils are not hearing the sounds in words or are unable to recall them in the correct order.	Morphological – errors due to a lack of awareness of morphemes can result in spellings such as 'trapt' for trapped, and 'ekscuse' for excuse.	Orthographical – errors include phonically plausible but inaccurate spellings such as 'gud' for good, and 'carm' for calm.
Possible teaching strategies	Explicit teaching of consonant and vowel phonemes. Practise sounding phonemes all the way through words. Focus on identification of common digraphs in words.	Focus on prefixes and suffixes and root words. Look at the relationship between meaning and spelling by looking at etymology. Teach common rules and generalisations for adding affixes, eg in– precedes most letters when creating negatives such as incorrect, but words beginning with b, m and p take im–, those beginning with l take il–, those beginning with r take ir–.	Practise GPCs. Look at patterns of letters and syllables within words. Encourage automatic recognition of whole words once they are accurately decoded.

Moats (accessed 2017)

Use this to keep a record of what worked well for you and what didn't. A strategy that works with one learner or group of learners may not work so well with another. Keeping a checklist helps you to work out what factors or learner characteristics call for one approach rather than another. There's a line at the bottom for you to add your own most frequently used strategy, if it's not already included in the list.

Strategy	Tried it with…	On… (date)	It worked	It didn't work	Worth trying again?
1. Understanding the challenges in English spelling					
2. Knowing the strategies good spellers use*					
3. How can you teach spellings?					
4. Understanding adjacent consonants					
5. CVCC words and how to teach them					
6. CCVC words and how to teach them					
7. How to teach morphology					
8. Understanding and teaching prefixes					
9. Understanding and teaching suffixes					
10. How to teach compound words					
11. Understanding spelling rules and generalisations					
Your own strategy?					

Introduction

Today we will look at teaching phonics at Key Stage 2. While some learners may have mastered the alphabetic code by the end of Key Stage 1 and be fluent readers, some will still be struggling with decoding and will require additional support. The pace of progress through phonics programmes at Key Stage 1 tends to be brisk and means that some learners may miss or misunderstand a crucial phase of systematic phonics teaching. The *KS2 Phonics Intervention Programme* (National Strategies, 2009, p 1) states that some learners may:

* experience difficulties with blending for reading and with segmenting for spelling;
* show confusion with certain graphemes and related phonemes;
* have difficulty segmenting longer words containing adjacent consonants;
* demonstrate a general insecurity with long vowel phonemes (for example, learners generally know the most common representation of a phoneme, such as /ai/ in *train*, but require more explanation and practice with the alternative spellings for any particular phoneme).

These shortcomings will prevent learners from reading for pleasure and meaning and may lead to disaffection with reading.

Today's strategies

* Developing an understanding of rhyme:
  1. Understanding the importance of rhyme
  2. Focusing on rhyming couplets
  3. Investigating rhymes
* Focusing on less common GPCs:
  4. Looking at national curriculum spelling lists
  5. Revisiting prefixes and suffixes
* Homophones:
  6. The challenge of homophones
* Homographs and homonyms, synonyms and antonyms
  7. Understanding homographs
  8. Understanding homonyms
  9. Using synonyms and antonyms

Activity: Back-to-front words

To understand how frustrating difficulties or confusion with reading might be, try reading the text below which is written with words in the right order, but with each word presented back-to-front (see end of section for the correct presentation).

> tI saw a gnol emit ecnis kcaJ dah neeb ot eht edisaes ni dnalgnE. yehT dah devil ta eht ymrA esab ni ynamreG rof a raey dna ti saw oot raf morf eht aes rof a yad tuo. ehT tsrif thgin eh deciton sa yeht deppets ffo eht sub saw eht gnikeirhs fo sllug. yehT deleehw dna dedilg evoba meht, tas no pmal stsop dna sgnidliub dna deppoh dnuora no eht dnuorg gnikool rof doof.

As you read, all of your focus is on decoding so it is difficult to derive meaning from the text. This is an extreme example because every word except 'a' is a challenge. For struggling readers there would be some words which they could read, but you can see how having to focus so strongly on word recognition at the expense of language comprehension might put learners off reading. It is vital, then, that teachers at Key Stage 2 have strategies for supporting struggling readers and don't simply regard phonics as something which Key Stage 1 teachers take care of. It is also important that those learners who are not succeeding in reading are still engaged with texts. This means taking into account that, while their reading ages may be below their chronological ages, they are still maturing and may not be interested in texts which were written for younger learners. It is vital that their interests are taken into account as well as their maturity levels when finding suitable texts. This may mean writing with them and for them so that they have things to read which interest them and enable them to see the value of reading.

However, phonics at Key Stage 2 is not simply for struggling readers: all learners will need to develop their phonic skills further as they meet new vocabulary and new subjects. It is important that they have strategies for decoding less common graphemes which will arise as they meet new topics and subject areas, and they will need lots more work on morphology as their vocabularies develop.

Engaging children's interest

Children who have struggled with literacy during Key Stage 1 may already be unenthusiastic about reading. It is important to look for ways to engage their interest and let them see that reading can be both entertaining and informative. By drawing upon their interests, teachers can support children's phonic development and reading comprehension skills. Simple activities are described below.

Sport

Collecting league tables and football results together with reports, programmes and magazines can enable you to create a range of engaging activities. Many children enjoy sport and have favourite teams and players. For some, who may have little interest in reading, the mere mention of Manchester United, Liverpool or Chelsea may be enough to gain their attention. They might be asked to match teams with similar phonemes or graphemes (eg **Ch**elsea and Man**ch**ester City) or make lists of clubs which include, say, digraphs in their names. They could create teams in which every player has to have a phoneme in her or his name which matches the club (eg La**ll**ana, Rona**l**do, Ba**l**e could play for Liverpool). They might also investigate grapheme-phoneme correspondences in the names of foreign players and discuss some of those which are the same as in English and some which are peculiar to other languages.

The examples above relate to football, but could just as easily be used for other sports such as cricket, athletics and rugby.

Popular music

Popular music can also be a source of interest for children, with exploration of musicians' names, song titles and, where appropriate, lyrics. They might work together to write their own lyrics to established tunes. This can involve discussion about rhyme and grapheme phoneme correspondences (see below).

Maps and charts

Maps and charts can be used to enable children to use their developing phonic awareness to identify place names and names of other items of interest. They might create their own maps and invent place names, discussing possible spellings and using an index to find real places with similar spellings. Children could even create posters advertising their invented places, using alliterative adjectives, for example, Delightful Dunford, Lovely Lowton and Fabulous Foxford.

Word cards

When reading a story to children, teachers can provide word cards for each child with key names and terms which will appear in a chapter. The words can be discussed in groups and as a class and then children can be asked to listen carefully to find out how their words are used in the story. At suitable points in the story, teachers can ask whose words have come up and in what context. There can be discussion about spelling as well as an emphasis on comprehension. Not only does this activity engage children's interest in stories, but it also broadens vocabulary and offers opportunities for retelling stories using the word cards as prompts.

As you read about the strategies described below, consider how you might incorporate children's interests in order to engage them and enable them to see reading as a meaningful activity.

Answer

It was a long time since Jack had been to the seaside in England. They had lived at the Army base in Germany for a year and it was too far from the sea for a day out. The first thing he noticed as they stepped off the bus was the shrieking of gulls. They wheeled and glided above them, sat on lamp posts and buildings and hopped around on the ground looking for food.

Strategy: Developing an understanding of rhyme

1. Understanding the importance of rhyme

Rhyme can introduce learners to a range of grapheme-phoneme correspondences (GPCs), while engaging them with texts. Hearing and seeing poems helps develop learners' phonemic awareness as well as their sense of rhyme.

2. Focusing on rhyming couplets

By focusing on rhyme, learners can develop an appreciation of variations in GPCs. Look at the rhyming couplets in the extract from Hilaire Belloc's *Jim* (note that the capital letters are placed where the poet placed them: at the beginning of each line and for every noun):

> There was a Boy whose name was Jim;
> His Friends were very good to him.
> They gave him Tea, and Cakes, and Jam,
> And slices of delicious Ham,
> And Chocolate with pink inside,
> And little Tricycles to ride,
> And read him Stories through and through,
> And even took him to the Zoo—
> But there it was the dreadful Fate
> Befell him, which I now relate.
> You know—at least you **ought** to know,
> For I have often told you so—
> That Children never are allowed

> To leave their Nurses in a Crowd;
> Now this was Jim's especial Foible,
> He ran away when he was able,
> And on this inauspicious day
> He slipped his hand and ran away!
> He hadn't gone a yard when—
> Bang!
> With open Jaws, a Lion sprang,
> And hungrily began to eat
> The Boy: beginning at his feet…

The first three rhymes are spelled in the same way, but these are followed by pairings such as *through* and *zoo*, *know* and *so*, *allowed* and *crowd*, *foible* and *able* (a near rhyme), and *eat* and *feet*. Although it is important that learners enjoy poems and engage with them, there is also an opportunity here to

A Spot of Theory

Research by Bryant et al (1990) involved testing 64 four-to six-year-olds' ability to detect rhyme at ages 4 years and 7 months and 5 years and 11 months. They were asked to pick the word which did not rhyme from three words accompanied by pictures, for example cat, hot, hat. *At 6 years 7 months, learners were given three different reading tests to assess their understanding of words and simple sentences, knowledge of frequent words, and spelling. It was found that those learners who had scored higher on the earlier rhyme tests also scored highly in the reading tests.*

discuss spelling patterns. One strategy could be to get two confident spellers to write the rhyming words on the board in separate columns as you read:

Jim	him
jam	ham
inside	ride
through	zoo
fate	relate
know	so
allowed	crowd
foible	able
bang	sprang

This can be followed by discussion, including about other words which would rhyme with those in the poem and their spelling patterns.

3. Investigating rhymes

Investigating rhymes might involve trying words out to see if they rhyme and then checking them in a dictionary, or it could be related to familiar names of people, places and objects. By engaging with rhyme in this way, learners can develop their vocabularies, improve their spelling and create a resource to support them when they write rhyming poetry.

Investigating rhymes

Samira wanted her Year 4 class to develop their ability to write rhyming poetry while improving their spelling. She had noticed that their earlier attempts at writing rhymes had often been rather contrived, with learners choosing vocabulary more for its ability to rhyme than for its ability to improve expression.

She created a bank of rhyming words and cut them up into individual word cards. She chose words which could have different spellings making the same rhyme:

stout	about	shirt	hurt	spring
thing	day	weigh	front	coat
note	hunt	thought	caught	hurry
worry	feed	lead	head	bed
doubt	court	chair	where	dare
wood	could	sky	high	buy

She devised various activities using the cards, including *snap* where learners turned their pile of cards over and if they made a rhyme they took a 'trick'. They also played a concentration game in which all the cards were face down and learners took turns to turn two over and take a 'trick' if they found a matching pair. Once learners were familiar with the words, Samira asked them to work as pairs with a dictionary to try to find as many words as they could which rhymed with each word.

The class went on to create a rhyming wall with words written on cards and learners were able to add further words as they found them in their reading.

Strategy: Focusing on less common GPCs

4. Looking at national curriculum spelling lists

At Key Stage 2 there are prescribed lists of spellings for learners to learn. Many of the words appear to have been chosen because they have the kinds of spellings which tend to challenge writers. There are several GPCs which may be unfamiliar to learners at the start of Year 3, but generally these GPCs can be found in other words, so developing a knowledge of, say, the /ks/ sound for the *cc* in *accident* will also help with words like *eccentric* and *accent*.

Activity: Year 3–4 spellings

Look at the words in the Year 3–4 list and decide:

💥 Which words might be taught together because they have GPCs in common?

💥 Which contain 'tricky' parts which will need to be focused upon?

Year 3–4 spellings in the national curriculum

accident	early	knowledge	purpose
actual	earth	learn	quarter
address	eight/eighth	length	question
answer	enough	library	recent
appear	exercise	material	regular
arrive	experience	medicine	reign

believe	experiment	mention	remember
bicycle	extreme	minute	sentence
breath	famous	natural	separate
breathe	favourite	naughty	special
build	February	notice	straight
busy/business	forward	occasion	strange
calendar	fruit	often	strength
caught	grammar	opposite	suppose
centre	group	ordinary	surprise
century	guard	particular	therefore
certain	guide	peculiar	though/although
circle	heard	perhaps	thought
complete	heart	popular	through
consider	height	position	various
continue	history	possess	weight
decide	imagine	possible	woman/women
describe	increase	potatoes	
different	important	pressure	
difficult	interest	probably	
disappear	island	promise	

(DfE, 2013, p 64)

You may have decided that *early*, *earth* and *learn* could be taught together because all contain the vowel trigraph *ear* pronounced as /ur/ in *turn*. You might group together all the words which include *–ough*, although as the pronunciation is different in each of *enough*, *though*, *thought* and *through* this may require caution, especially as *–ough* is a quadgraph in all but *enough* where it is two phonemes.

It is interesting that *favourite* and *centre* are spelled differently in US English (*favorite* and *center*), showing that grapheme variations sometimes exist between versions of Standard English.

5. Revisiting prefixes and suffixes

On Day 6 you looked at the addition of prefixes and suffixes. When working with older learners, it is important to make use of the knowledge they have gained about morphology when teaching the national curriculum spelling lists. By talking about the words and looking at the words which can be derived from them by adding prefixes and suffixes, you can develop their understanding of word-building, enhance their vocabularies and give them strategies for decoding new words.

Activity: Finding words which cannot be modified with prefixes and/or suffixes

A   Look at the first row of words in the Year 3–4 spelling list: *accident*, *early*, *knowledge* and *purpose*. Try adding prefixes and/or suffixes to each and see how many words you can make. For example, *accident* could become *accidents*, *accidental*, *accidentally*, *non-accidental*.

B   Next, look through the full list of spellings to see if there are any words which *cannot* be modified by adding prefixes and/or suffixes.

A Spot of Theory

Adoniou (2013, p 145) maintains that when learners build words using morphemes, this leads to improved spelling and increases learners' vocabulary knowledge. Adoniou uses the word breakfast *as an example and states:* 'if you understand that it means to **break a fast** after a night of not eating then you are less likely to spell it as "brekfast" '.

Adoniou maintains that an understanding of morphemes can help widen vocabulary and develop learners' understanding of how words work. This understanding can be further developed by focusing on different types of words and their spellings and meanings.

Answers

A   *Enough*, *therefore* and *perhaps* cannot be modified.

B   *Potatoes* has already been modified and the list gives *although* as a modification of *though*. Some people suggest that *February* cannot be modified, but you can live through many *Februaries*!

Strategy: Homophones

6. The challenge of homophones

Look at the words below. If you simply read them to a friend or a group of learners, how many do you think they would spell correctly?

sew	whole	where	yew	fate
sea	knead	rowed	their	buy

The answers you might get could include:

so or sow	see
hole	need
wear or ware	road
you	there
fete	by or bye

Of course, the first question most people would ask if invited to spell any of the words above would be something like 'Which *so* do you mean?'. Context is important in spelling because English has lots of *homophones*: words which sound the same as each other but have different spellings and meanings. These are the basis for many of our jokes (*What's black and white and red/read all over? A newspaper* etc), but they also cause problems when we are spelling. In this section, we will look at strategies to help learners cope with homophones. Homophone comes from the Greek words *homos*, meaning 'the same' and *phone*, meaning 'sound'.

A Spot of Theory

Dombey (2009) maintains that we are primed to recognise particular words and establish their meaning because we have an expectation due to the context in which we meet them. So if we look at a train timetable and see the word Reading, *we think of a place rather than an activity with books and pronounce it accordingly.*

Crystal (2012) argues that when homophones are taught together, this can be confusing and so you need to think carefully about when you teach homophones together and when you teach them with other words with similar spellings. So you might, for example, teach:

- *there with here and where – as they are all words connected with place and have a similar spelling pattern;*

- *their with heir and an explanation that this is an unusual way of spelling the /air/ phoneme;*

- *they're in the context of contractions, such as I'm, you're, he's, she's, we're;*

- *lead (the metal) with bread, dead, head;*

- *led (the verb, past tense) with fed, shed, bed;*

- *pair with fair, hair, stairs.*

This may be appropriate for weaker spellers, but good spellers may enjoy collecting homophones and find it easier to distinguish between spellings and meanings.

Near homophones

Some words sound almost the same, especially in some accents. For example, in many areas of England *are* and *our* have very similar pronunciations and this can lead to confusion when learners are writing, for example: *We put are coats on.*

There are lots of homophones in English. Below you can see some of the common English homophones and near homophones which learners may meet in Key Stages 1 and 2.

ate, eight	hour, our	sea, see
bare, bear	knew, new	sew, so, sow
be, bee	knot, not	some, sum
beach, beech	know, no	son, sun
bean, been	lessen, lesson	tale, tail
blew, blue	mail, male	there, their, they're
buy, by	meat, meet	threw, through
caught, court	pair, pare, pear	tire, tyre
cheap, cheep	pause, paws, pours	to, too, two
dear, deer	peace, piece	wait, weight
flour, flower	plain, plane	wear, where
for, fore, four	praise, prays, preys	way, weigh, whey
hear, here	read, red	weak, week
hi, high	right, write	which, witch
him, hymn	saw, soar, sore	wood, would

Faisal was concerned that many of the learners in his Year 3 class frequently misspelled homophones. He was mindful of research which showed that lower-ability spellers might find learning pairs of homophones confusing and so decided that he would do a homophone activity with the whole class but would adapt it for some learners during independent work.

Faisal made cards, placed them in magnetic holders and put them on the board and then asked learners to spot and match the pairs of words. For example:

weather	whether	way	weigh
hare	hair	eight	ate
hole	whole	mail	male
write	right	flower	flour
bored	board	groan	grown
eye	I	hear	here

Once learners had identified homophones (for example, *grown* and *groan*), he asked them to look closely at the spellings and to devise ways in which to remember spellings and to think of other words with the same spelling patterns, for example *groan*: *moan, loan*. He provided dictionaries so that learners could check that words existed and, if necessary, find out their meanings.

All learners took part, but Faisal made use of the words which had been found with similar spelling patterns to help his lower-ability spellers to learn spellings, for example they learned *hear, fear, dear* and *rear* together.

Strategy: Homographs and homonyms, synonyms and antonyms

Four other types of word present both challenges and opportunities at Key Stage 2: homographs, homonyms, synonyms and antonyms.

7. Understanding homographs

Homographs are words which are spelled the same but which sound different, for example:

" *I will record my new vinyl record.*

" *I refuse to use the new refuse bin.*

" *I was too close to the door to close it.*

The challenge when encountering homographs is to know how to pronounce words and so, as with homophones, context is crucial. By providing sentences, both orally and in writing, discussions can be prompted.

8. Understanding homonyms

Homonyms have different meanings, but the same sound and spelling. There are lots of homonyms in English, for example:

bank	bark	bat
bear	can	down
fine	fair	light
park	quarry	rock
rose	saw	

Like homographs, homonyms don't pose special problems for spelling, but can be discussed as part of vocabulary development. They are also the basis for many jokes which involve misunderstandings, for example:

" *How do you make a sausage roll? – Push it down a hill.*

" *Why did Rachel take the pencil to bed? – So that she could draw the curtains.*

Learners can be asked to make collections of homographs and homonyms and this can be a good way to involve parents and carers. Not only can this engage learners with spellings, but it can also enhance their vocabularies and help develop an interest in words. They might even be asked to find or make up jokes based upon homonyms and homophones.

9. Using synonyms and antonyms

Many classrooms have displays of vocabulary, including charts showing synonyms and antonyms. For Year 6, the national curriculum for England requires that learners learn: *'How words are related by meaning as synonyms and antonyms [for example, big, large, little]'* (DfE, 2013, p 78). By having a resource to draw upon, both teachers and learners can discuss vocabulary and talk about word-building and spelling.

Synonyms are words which have the same or very similar meanings, while antonyms are opposites. The example below is taken from a Year 5 classroom and is a resource learners use in writing lessons when they wish to vary their vocabulary.

Gemma introduced a synonym resource to her Year 5 class to enable them to broaden their vocabularies and use more diverse language when writing. During writing lessons, learners were encouraged to go to the wallets holding synonym cards when they wanted to vary the words they used.

Chart from Miss Gemma Ferguson's classroom at Archibald Primary, Middlesbrough.

Antonyms are often created by adding prefixes such as *un–* (*unlike*), *dis–* (*distaste*), *non–* (*non-accidental*) and *de–* (*defuse*) to make a word mean the opposite. Studying them can both enhance vocabulary and reinforce phonic and morphological understanding. A starting point for exploring antonyms can be oral, with learners asked to think of opposites such as *good* and *bad*, *high* and *low*, *heavy* and *light*. Where there could be more than one antonym, learners should be encouraged to think of what others might be used. This will usually lead to them citing words with prefixes.

You saw a range of prefixes on Day 6. Some of these can be used to create antonyms and can be the focus of lessons on spelling and vocabulary. In particular, you might look at:

anti–, de–, dis–, ex–, il–, im–, in–, mis–, non–, pre–, pro–, post– and un–

Because of the consistency of the spellings of prefixes, learners can learn new vocabulary and develop their confidence in spelling longer words.

Checklist

Use this to keep a record of what worked well for you and what didn't. A strategy that works with one learner or group of learners may not work so well with another. Keeping a checklist helps you to work out what factors or learner characteristics call for one approach rather than another. There's a line at the bottom for you to add your own most frequently used strategy, if it's not already included in the list.

Strategy	Tried it with...	On... (date)	It worked	It didn't work	Worth trying again?
1. Understanding the importance of rhyme					
2. Focusing on rhyming couplets					
3. Investigating rhymes					
4. Looking at national curriculum spelling lists*					
5. Revisiting prefixes and suffixes					
6. The challenge of homophones					
7. Understanding homographs					
8. Understanding homonyms					
9. Using synonyms and antonyms					
Your own strategy?					

Further reading

Adams, M J (1990) *Beginning to Read: Thinking and Learning about Print.* Cambridge: MIT Press.

Adoniou, M (2013) What Should Teachers Know About Spelling? *Literacy,* 48(3): 144–54. [online] Available at: http://onlinelibrary.wiley.com/doi/10.1111/lit.12017/abstract (accessed 7 May 2017).

Bald, J (2007) *Using Phonics to Teach Reading and Spelling.* London: Paul Chapman Publishing.

Bowen, C (2011) Table 3: Elimination of Phonological Processes. [online] Available at: http://speech-language-therapy.com/~speech/index.php?option=com_content&view=article&id=31:table3&catid=11:admin&Itemid=117 (accessed 1 May 2017).

Bryant, P E, MacLean, M, Bradley, L and Crossland, J (1990) Rhyme and Alliteration, Phoneme Detection, and Learning to Read. *Developmental Psychology,* 26(3): 429–38.

Crystal, B and Crystal, D (2014) *You Say Potato: A Book About Accents.* London: Macmillan.

Crystal, D (2005) *How Language Works.* London: Penguin.

Crystal, D (2009) The Words in the Mental Cupboard, in Gall, C. *BBC News Magazine.* [online] Available at: http://news.bbc.co.uk/1/hi/magazine/8013859.stm (accessed 6 May 2017).

Crystal, D (2012) *Spell It Out: The Singular Story of English Spelling.* London: Profile Books.

Cunningham, P and Cunningham, J (2002) What We Know About How to Teach Phonics, in Farstrup, A and Samuels, S J (eds) *What Research Has to Say about Reading*, pp 186–214. Delaware, NE: International Reading Association.

Davis, A (2013) To Read or Not to Read: Decoding Synthetic Phonics. *Impact: Philosophical Perspectives on Education Policy,* 20: 1–38.

DCSF (2009) *Support for Spelling.* London: DCSF.

DfE (2011a) *Teachers' Standards in England from September 2012.* London: DfE.

DfE (2011b) *Criteria for Assuring High-quality Phonic Work.* Runcorn: DfE. [online] Available at: www.education.gov.uk/schools/teachingandlearning/pedagogy/phonics/a0010240/criteria-for-assuring-high-quality-phonic-work (accessed 20 June 2017).

DfE (2013) *The National Curriculum in England.* London: DfE.

DfES (2007) *Letters and Sounds: Principles and Practice of High Quality Phonics.* London: DfES.

Dombey, H (2006) Phonics and English Orthography, in Lewis, M and Ellis, S (eds) *Phonics Practice, Research and Policy*. London: Paul Chapman, pp 95–104.

Dombey, H (2009) *Readings for Discussion – The Simple View of Reading.* [online] Available at: http://citeseerx.ist.psu.edu/viewdoc/download?doi=10.1.1.430.2749&rep=rep1&type=pdf (accessed 21 July 2017).

Gill, A and Waugh, D (2016) That Doesn't Sound Right – Teaching Common Exception Words in KS1. *Teach Reading and Writing.* Norfolk: Maze Media.

Glazzard, J and Stokes, J (2013) *Teaching Synthetic Phonics and Early English.* Northwich: Critical Publishing Ltd.

Hepplewhite, D (2007) *Simple to Complex Alphabetic Code Overview.* Phonics International.

Jackson, H (1995) *Words and their Meaning.* Harlow: Longman.

Johnston, R and Watson, J (2007) *Teaching Synthetic Phonics.* Exeter: Learning Matters.

Johnston, R, McGeown, S and Watson, J , (2012) Long-Term Effects of Synthetic Versus Analytic Phonics Teaching on the Reading and Spelling Ability of 10 Year Old Boys and Girls. *Reading and Writing,* 25(6): 1365–1384.

Jolliffe, W (2012) *Quick Fix for Phonics.* Witney: Scholastic.

Jolliffe, W and Waugh, D with Carss, A (2015) *Teaching Systematic Synthetic Phonics in Primary Schools* (2nd ed). London: Sage.

Kress, G (2000) *Early Spelling: Between Convention and Creativity.* London: Routledge.

Levy, R (2009) Children's Perceptions of Reading and the Use of Reading Scheme Texts. *Cambridge Journal of Education,* 39(3): 361–77. doi:10.1080/03057640903103769

Lloyd, S (1992) *The Phonics Handbook.* Chigwell: Jolly Learning.

Masterson, J, Stuart, M, Dixon, M and Lovejoy, S (2003) *Children's Printed Word Database*. Economic and Social Research Council funded project (Ref R00023406). Nottingham: DCSF.

McGuinness, D (2004) *Early Reading Instruction: What Science Really Tells Us about How to Teach Reading.* Cambridge, MA: MIT Press.

Medwell, J and Wray, D with Moore, G and Griffiths, V (2014) *Primary English Knowledge and Understanding* (7th ed). London: Sage.

Miskin, R (2011) *Read Write Inc.: Phonics Handbook.* Oxford: Oxford University Press.

Moats, L, *Looking Beyond Standardized Test Scores: Spelling Error Analysis for Planning Intervention.* [online] Available at: www.region10.org/r10website/assets/File/Beyond%20Standardized%20Test%20Scores%20Handout%20Louisa%20Moats.pdf (accessed 5 May 2017).

National Strategies (2009) *KS2 Phonics Intervention Programme.* London: National Strategies.

Nunes, T and Bryant, P (2006) *Improving Literacy through Teaching Morphemes.* London: Routledge.

Ofsted (2010) *Reading by Six.* London: Paul Chapman.

Rose, J (2006) *Independent Review of the Teaching of Early Reading, Final Report, March 2006* (The Rose Review – Ref: 0201-2006DOC-EN). Nottingham: DfES Publications.

Seymour, P, Aro, M and Erskine, J (2003) Foundation Literacy Acquisition in European Orthographies. *British Journal of Psychology*, 94: 143–74.

Siegel, L (2008) Phonological Processing Deficits and Reading Disabilities, in Metsala, J and Ehri, L (eds) *Word Recognition in Beginning Literacy*. Mahwah, NJ: Lawrence Erlbaum, pp. 141–60.

Snell, J and Andrews, R (2016) To What Extent Does a Regional Dialect and Accent Impact on the Development of Reading and Writing Skills? *Cambridge Journal of Education*. doi: 10.1080/0305764X.2016.1159660

Stevenson, A (ed) (2010) *Oxford English Dictionary* (3rd ed). Oxford: Oxford University Press.

Stuart, M (2006) Learning to Read the Words on the Page: The Crucial Role of Early Phonics Teaching, in Lewis, M and Ellis, S (eds) *Phonics: Practice, Research and Policy*, pp 19–29. London: PCP.

Tickell, C (2011) *The Early Years: Foundations for Life, Health and Learning* (The Tickell Review). Runcorn: DfE. [online] Available at: www.education.gov.uk/tickellreview (accessed 20 June 2017).

Torgerson, C J, Brooks, G and Hall, J (2006) *A Systematic Review of the Research Literature on the Use of Phonics in the Teaching of Reading and Spelling.* London: DfES.

Waugh, D, Carter, J and Desmond, C (2015) *Lessons in Teaching Phonics in Primary Schools.* London: Sage.

Waugh, D and Gill, A (2016) Tricky Customers – Teaching Common Exception Words in KS2. *Teach Reading and Writing.* Norfolk: Maze Media.

Whitehead, M (2007) *Developing Language and Literacy with Young Children.* London: Paul Chapman.

Williams, M (2006) 'Playing with Words': Level Work Including Vocabulary, Phonics and Spelling, in Fisher, R and Williams, M (eds) *Unlocking Literacy: A Guide for Teachers* (2nd ed), pp 40–50. London: Fulton.

Wyse, D and Goswami, U (2008) Synthetic Phonics and the Teaching of Reading. *British Education Research Journal,* 34(6): 691–710.

Glossary

TERM	DEFINITION AND EXAMPLES
Adjacent consonants	Consonants which appear next to each other in a word and can be blended together, eg *fl* in *flip*, *tr* in *track* (note that the *ck* in *track* is a digraph as the consonants come together to form a single sound or phoneme).
Alliteration	A sequence of words beginning with the same sound, eg *Daring Doncaster dash Derby's dreams*.
Analytic phonics	Children apply what they know about the patterns of letters and sounds in one word to others with similar structures, eg they might learn *black*, *track*, *crack* and *back* together.
Antonym	Antonyms are words which have opposite meanings, such as *good* and *bad*, *light* and *dark*. Some antonyms are created by adding a prefix, such as *happy* and *unhappy*, *legal* and *illegal*.
Blend	A combination of letters where individual letters retain their sounds.
Blending	To draw individual sounds together to pronounce a word, eg /f/l/a/p/, blended together, reads *flap*.
Common exception words	When teaching systematic synthetic phonics, we refer to common words with phonic irregularities as *common exception words*, eg *once*, *was*, *could*. These are often also referred to as words that have 'tricky bits'.
Decodable	Words which can be easily decoded using phonic strategies, eg *big*, *log*, *slip*, *trip*.
Decoding	The act of translating graphemes into phonemes, ie reading.
Digraph	Two letters which combine to make a new sound, eg *ch*, *sh*, *ph*.
Encoding	The act of transcribing units of sound or phonemes into graphemes, ie spelling.
Etymology	The origins of the formation of a word and its meaning.
Grapheme	A letter, or combination of letters that represent a phoneme.
Homographs	Words which are spelled the same but pronounced differently according to context, eg *She broke the record! I'll record Friends and listen to it later.*
Homonyms	Words which are spelled and pronounced in the same way but have different meanings, eg *I can't bear it* and *A brown bear*.
Homophones	Words which sound the same but have different spellings and meanings, eg *way* and *weigh*, *I* and *eye*, *sow*, *sew* and *so*.
Initial consonant blend	The consonants retain their original sounds but are blended together, as in *slug*.
Kinaesthetic	Learn using some form of physical (kinaesthetic) activity: for example, the use of actions to accompany phonemes and graphemes in *Jolly Phonics*.
Long vowel phonemes	The long vowel sounds as in *cool* or *gold*.
Mnemonic	A device for remembering something, such as *There is a rat in separate* (sep**arat**e).

Monosyllabic word	Word with one syllable, eg *dog*, *trap*, *foot*, *fool*.
Morpheme	The smallest unit of meaning, eg *like* is a single morpheme, but we could add the suffix *–ly* to make *likely*, and go on to add the prefix *un–* to make *unlikely*, which has three morphemes.
Multi-sensory	Use of a range of senses (hearing, seeing, feeling, moving).
Orthographic system	The spelling system of a language, ie the ways in which graphemes and phonemes relate to each other. The English orthographic system is more complex than many languages, since most phonemes can be represented by more than one grapheme.
Orthography	*Standardised spelling* – the sounds of a language represented by written or printed symbols.
Phoneme	The smallest single identifiable sound, eg the letters *ch* representing one sound.
Phonetics	The articulation and acoustic features of speech sounds. It explains the distinction between consonants and vowels and can help listeners identify the phonemic pattern of words.
Prefix	Morpheme or affix placed before a word to modify its meaning, eg *re–* in *remove*, *in–* in *insecure*.
Quadgraph	Four letters that combine to make one sound, eg *augh* in *caught*, *ough* in *though*.
Rhyme	Words that sound the same but do not necessarily share the same spelling, eg *great* and *rate*, *buy* and *sigh*, *try* and *cry*.
Segmenting	Splitting up a word into its individual phonemes in order to spell it, ie the word *cat* has three phonemes: /c/a/t/.
Split digraph	Two letters, which are not adjacent, making one sound, eg *a–e* as in *cake*, *o–e* as in *hole*, *i–e* as in *bite*, *e–e* as in *these*, *u–e* as in *cube*.
Suffix	Morpheme or affix added to a word to modify its meaning, eg *–ful* in *useful*, *–ed* in *stamped*.
Syllable	A unit of pronunciation having one vowel sound. This can be taught by identifying 'beats' in a word through clapping or putting a hand flat underneath your chin and then saying a word can help, as every time the hand moves, it represents another syllable.
Synonym	Words which have the same or very similar meanings are synonyms, eg *tasty* and *delicious*, *simple* and *easy*.
Synthetic phonics	Words are separated into individual phonemes and then blended together to read the word, eg /b/l/e/n/d/. This compares with *analytic phonics* in which segments or parts of words are analysed and patterns are compared with other words, eg /bl/end/ and /sp/end/.
Tricky words	When teaching systematic synthetic phonics, we sometimes refer to common words with phonic irregularities as 'tricky words', eg *once*, *was*, *could*. Many of the most common words have exceptions to common grapheme–phoneme correspondences. Such words are now referred to as *common exception words* in the national curriculum.
Trigraph	Three letters which combine to make a new sound, eg *augh* in *caught* and *ough* in *though*.